The Internet literacy handbook

2nd edition

Compiled by
Janice Richardson (editor),
Andrea Milwood Hargrave, Basil Moratille,
Sanna Vahtivouri, Dominic Venter and Rene de Vries

Updated by
Betsy Burdick, Chris Coakley
and Janice Richardson

Media Division
Directorate General II – Human Rights

Good Governance in the Information Society Project
Directorate General of Political Affairs

Council of Europe

French edition:

Maîtrise d'Internet – Manuel

ISBN-10: 92-871-5938-6
ISBN-13: 978-92-871-5938-0

Cover: Graphic Design Workshop, Council of Europe

Council of Europe
F-67075 Strasbourg Cedex

ISBN-10: 92-871-5939-4
ISBN-13: 978-92-871-5939-7

Printed in Belgium

Contents

Tips for the reader ... 5

Introduction ... 7

Fact Sheet 1 – Getting connected ... 9

Fact Sheet 2 – Setting up websites ... 11

Fact Sheet 3 – Searching for information ... 15

Fact Sheet 4 – Portals ... 19

Fact Sheet 5 – E-mail ... 23

Fact Sheet 6 – Spam ... 27

Fact Sheet 7 – Chat ... 31

Fact Sheet 8 – Newsgroups ... 37

Fact Sheet 9 – World-wide libraries ... 39

Fact Sheet 10 – Music and images on the Internet ... 43

Fact Sheet 11 – Creativity ... 47

Fact Sheet 12 – Games ... 51

Fact Sheet 13 – Distance learning ... 55

Fact Sheet 14 – Labelling and filtering ... 59

Fact Sheet 15 – Privacy ... 63

Fact Sheet 16 – Security ... 67

Fact Sheet 17 – Bullying and harassment ... 71

Fact Sheet 18 – Shopping online ... 75

Fact Sheet 19 – Becoming an active e-citizen ... 77

Fact Sheet 20 – Mobile technology ... 81

Fact Sheet 21 – Blogs ... 85

Tips for the reader

1. For an explanation of the terms used in this handbook, the authors refer you to Wikipedia – a free-content encyclopaedia, written collaboratively by users from around the world, and which is constantly updated. The handbook provides web addresses that will take you directly to many specific terms in Wikipedia, such as "Boolean search", "zombie computer" or "phishing" to name but a few; others can be found via the Wikipedia home page at <http://www.wikipedia.org>. Wikipedia definition addresses are encased in (parentheses). Other website addresses are encased in <brackets>.

Please note that Wikipedia references link directly to the English language version of the Wikipedia website, which offers a number of other language versions to choose from.

2. To avoid having to type out lengthy and cumbersome Web addresses cited in this handbook, consult the online version, which provides automatic links. It can be accessed at <http://www.coe.int/media>. Consult it as well for any Web addresses that you are unable to open.

3. The handbook uses the term "student" throughout. It refers to any young person, whether a student, school student or pupil, who is learning in a school or at home, irregardless of age or level.

All Internet addresses cited were last accessed in January 2006.

Introduction

Why create Internet literacy fact sheets?

Over the past decade or so, the Internet and mobile technology have transformed multiple facets of life in society across the world. They have changed our work and leisure patterns and they place greater demands on us as active citizens.

The Council of Europe's Internet literacy fact sheets are intended as an aid and a guide in using this remarkable network of information and communication. The aim is to:

- offer teachers and parents sufficient technical know-how to allow them to share young people's and children's voyages of discovery through communication technology;
- highlight ethical issues and give insight into added-value in education;
- provide ideas for constructive, practical activities in class or at home to draw benefits from the Internet and mobile technology;
- share best practice in widely varying domains of Internet use;
- provide links that will give further information or practical examples.

Ethical issues and dangers on the Internet

As we point out in each fact sheet, alongside the many advantages the Internet has brought, we must also respond to certain challenges. Viruses (http://en.wikipedia.org/wiki/Computer_virus), for example, cost administrations and private enterprise in Europe alone some two to three billion euros annually. Unsolicited e-mails, otherwise known as spam (http://en.wikipedia.org/wiki/E-mail_spam), now account for almost 90% of all e-mails, with more than 1.5% containing malicious code. A significant percentage of content on the Internet is either illicit or prejudicial, undermining the very basis of human rights and human dignity. Furthermore, that permanently fragile concept of equality is once again under threat as the digital divide (http://en.wikipedia.org/wiki/Digital_divide) separates the information "haves" and "have nots". Many young people are experiencing a growing disadvantage due to lack of material means to access the Internet, technical skills and online skills to search for information and use it effectively.

Getting the most out of information and communication technology

The Internet is, as its name indicates, no more than a route between information networks. Already access means are changing with the development of new technology such as wireless networking and 3G mobile services.

Nowadays every citizen needs to be information literate, a 21st-century form of literacy built upon the four fundamental pillars of education which constitute the very foundations of society. These are learning to know, to do, to be and to live together.

An evolving manual to respond to teacher and parent needs

As technologies evolve and other information sources become available, these fact sheets will be updated and new ones added. You are welcome to participate in this project by sending us your feedback or your ideas on classroom activities, best practice or pertinent links. Please send your contribution to the Council of Europe at: media.IS@coe.int

Fact Sheet 1

Getting connected

The Internet is a worldwide network of computers linked together through servers which function as connection nodes (http://en.wikipedia.org/wiki/Node_%28 networking%29). In March 2005 there were an estimated 900 million Internet users in the world of which more than 250 million were in Europe.

Educational benefits

- The Internet offers a wealth of new ideas and resources for teachers. Lesson plans, online exercises for students and electronic educational games.
- The Internet facilitates exchange of experience and communication between teachers and students across international borders.
- The Internet provides students with the opportunity to take part in projects to practise language and share cultures. This can be quicker and more efficient than traditional pen pal exchanges and does not involve the expense of a school trip.
- The Internet makes research tools accessible even to those who do not regularly visit a traditional library.

Ethical considerations and risks

- As in the offline world, there is fraud, false information and inappropriate material for children.
- While Internet offers a number of new possibilities, technical solutions are not always better than traditional ones. For example, e-mail has revolutionised communication, but it will never replace face-to-face communication.

How to

- If you are connecting from an institution (school, university, administration) your computer is probably automatically linked to an in-house server.
- To get connected to the Internet from home, you will need:

  - a computer equipped with a modem;

  - a telephone connection;

  - a subscription to an Internet service provider (ISP).
- ISPs (http://en.wikipedia.org/wiki/Internet_service_provider) form the necessary link between the user and the Internet. They can be private companies such as telecom or cable companies, or organisations such as universities.

- ISPs usually require a monthly subscription fee, and offer a range of services.
- A dialup (http://en.wikipedia.org/wiki/Dial-up_access) connection allows the user to access the Internet through a standard analogue telephone line. The user is often charged according to time connected, as with a normal phone call. An analogue line does not allow an Internet connection and phone connection at the same time. Connection speeds are slow.
- A broadband (http://en.wikipedia.org/wiki/Broadband_Internet_access) connection provides access through a digital line. ISDN (http://en.wikipedia.org/wiki/ISDN) and DSL (http://en.wikipedia.org/wiki/Digital_Subscriber_Line) are examples. ISPs' broadband subscriptions usually allow unlimited access time for a fixed fee. However, a cap may be set on how much data can be downloaded. Connection speeds are much faster and these lines allow a phone to be used without the need to disconnect the Internet.
- An increasing number of computers, especially laptops, are fitted with wireless network cards (Wifi) (http://en.wikipedia.org/wiki/wifi). These allow cable-free access to the Internet at home or at "wireless hotspots". Wireless hotspots can be found at public places such as cafés and airports.

Best practice

- Choose a connection appropriate for your Internet usage. A broadband connection is likely to be worthwhile if you use the Internet regularly.
- If you have broadband, do not remain connected unless you are using it. It may not cost extra money, but it increases the security risk to your data (see Fact Sheet 16 on security).
- Draw up an acceptable use policy (AUP) (http://en.wikipedia.org/wiki/AUP) if others will be using the computer or network you are responsible for.

For further information

- The List is a worldwide directory of ISPs: <http://www.thelist.com/>.
- Education websites such as European Schoolnet at <http://www.eun.org/ portal/ index.htm>, Global Schoolhouse at <http://www.globalschoolnet.org/GSH/> and Education World at <http://www.educationworld.com/> offer resources and collaborative projects.
- Advice on writing an AUP from can be obtained from Becta, the UK agency for ICT in education: <http://www.ictadvice.org.uk/index.php?section=ap&catcode=as_pl_acc_03&rid=1963&rr=1&PHPSESSID=820174b4b4df8ca7de75604c566d00ee>.
- The Insafe portal offers resources and advice on how to get connected and surf safely: <http://www.saferinternet.org/ww/en/pub/insafe/>.

Fact Sheet 2

Setting up websites

So you want to set up a website?

School administrators, teachers and students increasingly feel the need to present their school and/or work on the World Wide Web – the growth in the amount of homepages is incredible. A good school website is a wonderful public relations tool that can be used in many different ways, for example for presenting school information or publishing lesson plans. It is also, of course, a very important pedagogical tool.

But since websites can be used in so many ways, it is sometimes overwhelming for administrators, teachers, students or parents who want to start their own website to know where to begin.

Before starting to build your own website, you should consider the following points:

- What is the purpose of your website?
- Why do you need a website?
- Who is your website audience – world, district, hometown or just students and parents?
- What will the content be?

Turning local schools into international schools

- The Internet makes it possible for students all over the world to communicate and collaborate very easily. Today's classroom defies the traditional image of a brick and mortar room in a fixed geographical location. When using the Internet as a communication tool, classroom walls disappear and local schools go global.
- A good school website is interactive and, by means of tools such as message boards (http://en.wikipedia.org/wiki/Message_boards), it is possible for students, parents and teachers to access the latest school information anytime anywhere.
- Students can play an active role in setting up websites. In fact, when we look at website contests like Think Quest at <http://www.thinkquest.org/>, CyberFair at <http://www.globalschoolnet.org/index.html> and others, websites made by lower and upper secondary school students are very often of a better quality then the websites made by teachers.

- Web-building basics can be taught as part of the curriculum: students can create websites as assignments for math, biology, language or music. In fact, all subject areas are compatible with website creation.
- The wonderful thing about the Internet is that students are not restricted to creating websites with their own classmates: they can collaborate with students from all over the world using communication tools like e-mail (http://en.wikipedia.org/wiki/Email), video conferencing (http://en.wikipedia.org/wiki/Video_conferencing) and chat (http://en.wikipedia.org/wiki/Chat).

For further information, take a closer look at Fact Sheet 7 on chat, 11 on creativity and 1 on getting connected.

Playing safe

It is important to consider safety issues when putting together any kind of school-related website.

- School policy on Internet safety and acceptable use must be clearly defined before creating an official website or having students participate in website-building competitions.
- The layout and the way photos are used should reflect school Internet safety policy.
- Because of safety and privacy concerns, many schools do not provide the names, or only give first names, of those in photos they publish. This is something to consider when you set up your website: what is your safety protocol in this matter?
- It is a good idea to screen all external hyperlinks to other websites in order to ensure integrity of information and that the websites adequately reflect the school's stance on Internet safety.
- Will you filter your Internet access or will you teach your students to be more "streetwise"? Many schools find a combination of these two techniques to be effective.
- When students create a website as an assignment, keep in mind that it can be visited by users from all over the world. Think of these websites as a kind of public relations tool for your school. Therefore it would be wise for teachers to supervise students' work and guide them during the creative process.
- Teachers are ultimately responsible for all work students produce. Therefore, teachers need to have the power to refuse web pages or remove them from a school or project website. In order to adequately supervise students' work, teachers should always have access to passwords (http://en.wikipedia.org/wiki/Password), websites (http://en.wikipedia.org/wiki/Website) and so forth.

Building a school website

When used correctly a school website can serve as a powerful tool to draw together the many different facets of a community. It can foster a sense of cohesion and is a valuable communication tool which makes information easily accessible to all parties. Here are some helpful suggestions for Web content.

- Teachers could provide lesson plans, or overviews of what students did during a certain period.
- Administrators might post schedules or announcements.
- Students may want to publish art, poems, stories, reports or other work.
- Parents can use the site to announce parent-teacher activities, such as festivals or other gatherings.
- The community-at-large may use it as a forum for announcements from or about soccer teams, field trips, police, road workers and so forth.

A wide variety of content may enrich a website, but a wide base of contributors can also make Web maintenance chaotic. It is important that a small team of people is chosen to be responsible for collecting and editing content. This task might be best carried out by a teacher or administrator or other person chosen to function as the information and communication technology (ICT) co-ordinator.

Some basic requirements to consider before website set-up are:

- Software: Most webmasters and web editors prefer to work with WYSIWYG (http://en.wikipedia.org/wiki/WYSIWYG) html editors such as Dreamweaver and FrontPage. These programs allow editing in a familiar environment without necessarily requiring the user to know html. Web content management systems are often used and some have been designed with schools in mind.
- Hardware: Modest hardware resources are helpful, such as image scanners (http://en.wikipedia.org/wiki/Image_scanner), digital photo cameras, digital video cameras, tripods and tape recorders.
- Hosting (http://en.wikipedia.org/wiki/Web_hosting): Schools need to find an organisation which will provide an online system for storing Web pages, images, files video and so forth and making them accessible via the web. It is important to research different providers and services offered to ensure that the plan meets your school's needs.

Best practice

Through trial and error, your school will develop a method to reach your target audience in an efficient manner. A model school website often includes:

- Contact information such as addresses and telephone numbers.
- Information about the school, for example lessons plans, care and so forth.
- Information about the staff.
- Information about the involvement of the parent-teacher organisations.
- Classroom pages with the latest information, drawings and photos from students.
- Links to related educational sites.
- A "guest book" for visitors to "sign".

Some technical considerations for best practice would include:

- A pleasant, easy-to-read design.
- Web accessibility compliance to cater to users with disabilities.

- Avoiding large graphics or other files that will take a lot of time to load.
- Consistent use of layout, easy navigation and information on when the last update was made.
- Versions in different languages when appropriate. English is often chosen as a common language when reaching out to students from different countries.
- A healthy respect for children's rights, social and cultural diversity, personal and physical integrity, and the democratic values of equality, freedom and friendship. For example, if students will be using your school website to connect with each other, it might be helpful to employ guidelines such as those published on Chatdanger: <http://www.chatdanger.com/>.

For further information

There are thousands of good websites that meet these standards: two examples are St Joan of Arc primary school in the United Kingdom at <http://www.st-joanarc.sefton.sch.uk/index.php> and the International School of Amsterdam in the Netherlands at <http://www.isa.nl/About/abouthome.html>. More information to help in building your school website can be found at:

- Building a School Website: <http://www.wigglebits.com/>.
- Education World – the Educator's best friend: <http://www.education-world.com/>.
- Webmonkey articles / tutorials for html, design and development: <http://webmonkey.wired.com/webmonkey/authoring/html_basics/>.
- Webmonkey for kids: <http://webmonkey.wired.com/webmonkey/kids/lessons/index.html>.
- "Lessons on teaching writing from website design". A University of Washington professor showcases ways that students can transfer skills used to build a website to the writing process: <http://www.newhorizons.org/strategies/literacy/stone.htm>.

Potential school partners and a wide variety of school websites can be found at:

- European Schoolnet's eTwinning action: <http://www.etwinning.net/ww/en/pub/etwinning/index2005.htm>.
- European Council of International Schools: <http://www.ecis.org/>.
- Directory of UK Schools websites: <http://www.schoolswebdirectory.co.uk/>.
- European Schools Project Association: <http://www.esp.uva.nl/>.

Fact Sheet 3

Searching for information

Introduction

The Internet is the source of an unprecedented amount of information, and is constantly changing and expanding. The first search engines (http://en.wikipedia.org/wiki/Search_ engine) for the Internet appeared in 1993.

Most searches work by collecting information about websites using an automatic web crawler (http://en.wikipedia.org/wiki/Web_crawler) which follows links and stores information about content. Many search engines check not only web pages but also online newsgroups (http://en.wikipedia.org/wiki/Newsgroup) and databases, and a search for the word "website" on the popular search engine Google at <http://www.google.com/> finds more than 1 billion results in 0.07 seconds.

Educational added value

- The Internet is an exceptional resource that allows quick and efficient research on any number of topics.
- The skills necessary to perform research on the Internet and in traditional libraries are similar. Successful searches require critical content analysis and Internet literacy.

Ethical considerations and risks

- Maintain a healthy scepticism about material you find. The Internet offers a free space for people to air opinions and put forward ideas. Be sure to evaluate with a critical eye in order to avoid propagating myths or falling for false claims.
- A number of websites offer complete essays on a wide variety of subjects for use by students. By using these files, students are misrepresenting their work and committing plagiarism.
- Be conscious of copyright issues if you use material you find on the Internet (see Fact Sheet 10 on music and images).
- As far as possible, credit the author and give the source of material you quote or use. This is important because:

  - it gives the author and source due credit;

  - it protects you from accusations of plagiarism;

  - it helps others form their own judgment about the credibility of the material.

- Websites use a variety of means, including payment, to improve their ranking in search engine results. Some search engines, such as Google, clearly identify which results are sponsored advertisements. Many others do not make this distinction.
- The most common search terms entered to search engines are used to find sexually explicit content. However, search engines generally censor these terms when listing the top searches performed on their websites.

How to

- The vast majority of people search for information on the Internet by using a search engine (http://en.wikipedia.org/wiki/Search_engine).
- A metasearch engine (http://en.wikipedia.org/wiki/Metasearch_engine) or "ferret" allows searching several search engines simultaneously.
- Search engines usually require the user to input a number of key words.
- "Boolean" (http://en.wikipedia.org/wiki/Boolean_datatype) searches can specify that key words appear together, or exclude results containing certain key words. These work slightly differently according to the search engine. Using quotation marks, plus and minus signs are the most common methods.
- Some search engines include directories which involve searching through categories and sub-categories.

Best practice

- Use specialist sites instead of standard searches. For example, when searching for the meaning of a word, use a dictionary such as <http://education. yahoo.com/reference/ dictionary/> site instead of search engine.
- Vary search terms. Different combinations of key words will bring out different results and a selection of searches will bring out more relevant results.
- Bookmark useful sites so you do not have to search for them again.
- If you find useful material, print or save it. You may not find it again or it may be taken offline without warning.
- Enclose specific phrases in quotation marks in order to narrow down searches and find exact matches.
- If you cannot find the answers through a search engine, post a query in a relevant newsgroup (see Fact Sheet 8 on newsgroups).

For further information

- The most popular search engines are Google: <http://www.google.com/>, Yahoo: <http://search.yahoo.com/> and MSN: <http://search.msn.com/>.
- Clusty at <http://clusty.com/> and Grokker at <http://www.grokker.com/> are innovative search tools with an alternative approach.
- Google Zeitgeist at <http://www.google.com/press/zeitgeist.html> shows the latest trends according to what searches people are making on Google.
- Wikipedia is a free-content encyclopaedia, written collaboratively by users from around the world: <http://www.wikipedia.org/>.

Fact Sheet 4

Portals

What is a portal?

Portals are websites that serve as a starting point to find targeted material or activities on the Internet. They provide the user with focused links and information specific to categories or areas of interest. Typically a portal appears as a web page with a map of links to topics or fields of interest. It often includes a search engine (http://en.wikipedia.org/wiki/Search_engine), chat (http://en.wikipedia.org/wiki/Chat), games (http://en.wikipedia.org/wiki/Online_gaming), news feeds (http://en.wikipedia.org/wiki/RSS_%28file_format%29) and content among other things.

Portals can be classified into two general types – horizontal and vertical.

Horizontal portals offer a broad range of services, activities and content. They can provide items such as news, weather, financial information and links to popular culture items, like movies or music, in addition to directories of links to specific topic areas. Yahoo! at <http://www.yahoo.com/> is probably the best known example.

Vertical portals provide a wide variety of content aimed at a specific type of user. A good example of an education-related vertical portal is the United Nations Educational Portal: <http://www.un.org/Pubs/chronicle/eosportal_index.asp>.

What are portals used for?

Portals function as a starting point for investigation into a topic. Searching the Internet for information is similar to using a traditional library. Searches must be done in a methodical way and a portal can assist you by breaking down topics into logical categories.

Portals offer a useful "at-a-glance" function for the range of topics within a theme. For example, within the subject of science, we can view various forms of biology, such as oceanography or botany. Similarly, the category of art history is an expansive field within the history category.

Ethical issues on portals

Portals are very often dependent on sponsorship or advertising, and will promote products and services accordingly. It is important to remember that the links offered by portals reflect the value sets of a particular group. Make sure that these values are acceptable to you for your students or children, before including them as a hyperlink on your website.

Some portals may require membership or registration, which may be paying. Before you register (even for "free" services) make sure that you understand the terms and conditions of the service, and that you have examined and understood the privacy policy of the website. See <http://www.netlingo.com/right.cfm?term =privacy%20policy>.

Continue using your critical thinking skills! It is a good idea to try new portal resources on a regular basis just to reinforce the information you receive from your shortlist of favourite standbys.

Following links from a portal may lead the unsuspecting user to sites that contain content, products or participatory processes inappropriate for your children or students. You can limit the "active" links according to your judgment using filtering software (http://en.wikipedia.org/wiki/Content_filtering_software) or settings in your browser.

Using portals for classroom activities

- Set a search target for any topic: create teams that use different portals, as well as a team that uses other search techniques described in Fact Sheet 3 on searching for information. Allow the teams to compare results, ease of access and quality of information.
- Create a topic for exploration, for example 18th-century art depicting children, or ecosystem dynamics of a particular species in the ocean.
- Provide your class with portal URLs (http://en.wikipedia.org/wiki/URL) that will lead to links supporting the lesson plan.
- As there will probably be too many links for individuals to follow, create teams to divide up the links and cover as many as possible, and allow each team to present their findings.
- Team results may differ, thus providing a narrower focus for further refinement of the class' learning.
- Create a portal for either of the above two subjects. This would involve creating a web page, defining the categories that emerge from your projects, creating the links that inform these categories, and testing the page with another class.

Best practice

- Be prepared: you need to take several steps before introducing portals into your school environment. Create a staff team to develop this resource for your particular needs.
- Identify the subject areas you wish your students to investigate with the use of portals.
- Now identify a range of portals, using search engines, for each subject area you are interested in.

- Apply an evaluation of each portal according to criteria agreed as policy in your school, or use the evaluation process guidelines in Fact Sheet 3.

In addition to evaluating information, you may also establish whether the service is free or not; what value system underpins the service; whether there are any cultural or language issues to be taken care of; if the site promotes or sells any products; if the site offers services such as e-mail or chat; and if you would want students to access these services (see "Best practice in Education Portals" below for an in-depth discussion).

- Make a selection of the best portals. Now explore these portals thoroughly, testing and evaluating links as you go. Make lists of problem areas, and filter inappropriate links.
- Remember to use the skills learned from Fact Sheet 3. Saving, referencing and cataloguing your process will make it easier to obtain a useful outcome.

For further information

- Yahoo! at <http://www.yahoo.com/>, Netscape at <http://www.netscape.com/>, Lycos at <http://www.netscape.com/>, Infospace at <http://www.infospace.com/> and About.com at <http://www.about.com/> are some of the most popular portals on the Web.
- The Education Portal at <http://www.theeducationportal.com/>, Discovery School at <http://school.discovery.com/schrockguide/index.html> and <http://www.thegateway.org/> are examples of educational portals with different approaches to design, usage and content.
- Best Practice in Education Portals: <http://www.col.org/Consultancies/02EducationPortals.htm>. This excellent in-depth evaluation report on education portals best-practice is worth reading for educators wishing to create viable policy criteria for portal usage in their school environment.
- Wonderport at <http://www.wonderport.com/> gives a breakdown of different types of portals including news, directories, reference and so forth.
- Art History Resources on the Web can be found at <http://witcombe.sbc.edu/ARTHLinks.html>. Christopher Witcombe's award-winning art history portal is worth a visit whatever your subject area.

Fact Sheet 5

E-mail

Introduction

E-mail (http://en.wikipedia.org/wiki/Email) short for electronic mail, is the system for sending messages between computers connected in a network such as the Internet. The term also refers to the message itself. An e-mail is usually transferred successfully in a matter of seconds and the recipient can access and reply whenever it is convenient. A flexible and efficient system, e-mail has drastically changed the way we work and communicate. Billions of messages are sent every day.

An e-mail address is composed of two parts: local and domain, separated by the "@" sign. The local name will often – but not always – indicate the name of a user. The domain will indicate their organisation, company or Internet service provider. Domain names may indicate type of organisation and/or country. For example, name@ox.ac.uk would be someone working or studying at Oxford University.

An e-mail message is divided into a header and a body. The header includes information about the sender, recipient(s), date and time, and a subject line. The body includes the main text of a message, perhaps with a "signature" including the sender's contact details.

E-mail can be sent and received via a mail user agent (MUA) (http://en.wikipedia.org/wiki/MUA). MUAs are computer applications that need to be installed on a computer. Although current messages can be accessed remotely, the mail program is usually used from the same location.

Another method for e-mail transmission is via webmail (http://en.wikipedia.org/wiki/Webmail), which allows the user to download and send e-mail from any computer that has an Internet connection. Messages are stored at a remote location and are therefore available regardless of the user's location.

Education

E-mail is increasingly being used as a channel of communication between teacher and student. For example, teachers can inform an entire group of upcoming changes or distribute and receive study material for distance learning (see Fact Sheet 13 on distance learning).

E-mail is a valuable tool in cross-cultural projects between classes of students in different countries. Students can use it to develop their language skills and share information about their cultures.

Some quiet and shy students express themselves better through e-mail than they would in face-to-face classroom discussion.

Ethical considerations and risks

- Discussion tends to be less formal in e-mail than it would be in a traditional written letter.
- The expression of emotions via e-mail is difficult. This problem can be solved through the use of small caricatures called "emoticons" (http://en.wikipedia.org/wiki/ Emoticons#Basic_examples). Use these sparingly, however, to keep from distracting from your message.
- A high proportion of e-mail sent is unsolicited and usually undesired spam (http://en. wikipedia.org/wiki/E-mail_spam). (see Fact Sheet 6 on spam).
- Apart from commercial spam, there is also an issue with e-mail sent between friends and colleagues. Some users copy in more people than are relevant to an issue, or distribute jokes and other such forwarded e-mails to those who may not want them.
- Some "forwards" are false or fraudulent. One example is where an e-mail claims to be tracked. Often citing a cause such as a sick child requiring surgery, it falsely claims that a company or organisation has promised that money will be paid each time it is forwarded.
- E-mail is the most common method for spreading malware (http://en.wikipedia.org/wiki/Malware) such as viruses (http://en.wikipedia.org/wiki/Computer_virus), and worms (http://en.wikipedia.org/wiki/Computer_worm).
- It is easy to conceal a name in order to be misleading. This can be done by simply changing the name in the settings or creating a webmail address such as elvispresley@hotmail.com. Even if you recognise the e-mail address, be aware that that the owner's machine may a "zombie computer" (http://en.wikipedia.org/wiki/Computer_ zombie) affected by a hacker or virus.
- A link may appear to be directing you to one website when in fact it leads to another. This is particularly common in phishing scams (http://en.wikipedia.org/wiki/Phishing).

Best practice

- Keep e-mails messages short and to the point. Try to avoid long blocks of text.
- Make sure you include relevant words in the subject line. This helps the recipient identify your message as being genuine and aids finding the mail at a later time.
- Be considerate in the volume of e-mail you send out. Use the "reply-to-all" facility only if the message is relevant for all, and avoid forwarding mails to those who may not appreciate it.

- Avoid checking your e-mails every 10 minutes. Many people allow e-mail to be a constant interruption.
- Think carefully before including private or sensitive information, such as bank details. E-mails can be intercepted and are easily forwarded.
- Use the "plain text only" setting in your e-mail. Html can allow for more attractive presentation but can also be used to spread malicious code.
- Maintain a healthy scepticism about e-mails you receive. Do not open e-mails if you do not trust the source.
- Be especially wary of attachments. If you were not expecting an attachment from the sender or do not trust it for any other reason, delete without opening.
- Be sure to consult Fact Sheet 6 on spam and 16 on security for additional advice on e-mail.

How to

- E-mail with a MUA (http://en.wikipedia.org/wiki/MUA) requires the program to be installed on your computer. Most computers come with a pre-installed MUA (http://en.wikipedia.org/wiki/MUA) such as Microsoft Outlook.
- Setting up a free web-based e-mail account is very simple. Popular webmail sites such as Yahoo! <http://mail.yahoo.com/> and Hotmail <http://login.passport.net/uilogin. srf?lc=1033&id=2> have a straightforward registration procedure.
- For information on setting up a spam filter see Fact Sheet 6.

For further information

- Well-known examples of MUAs are Microsoft Outlook: <http://office.microsoft.com/en-gb/FX010857931033.aspx> or Mozilla Thunderbird: <http://www.mozilla.org/projects/thunderbird/>.
- Two of the most popular webmail sites are MSN Hotmail: <http://login.passport.net/uilogin.srf?lc=1033&id=2> and Google's Gmail.
- OECD page on spam: <http://www.oecd.org/department/0,2688,en_2649_22555297_1_1_1_1_1,00.html>.
- BBC article: "Time to switch off and slow down": <http://news.bbc.co.uk/2/hi/technology/4682123.stm>.
- Truth or Fiction is a website for Internet users to check the veracity of commonly forwarded e-mails: <http://www.truthorfiction.com/>.

Fact Sheet 6

Spam

Introduction

Spam refers to the mass mailing of unsolicited messages to multiple recipients. It is most commonly associated with e-mail, but also applies to newsgroups, instant messaging and so forth.

Different countries have different legal definitions for spam and use different approaches to counter it. The Organisation for Economic Co-operation and Development (OECD) has put together a task force to try and homologise these approaches: see <http://www.oecd.org/ department/0,2688,en_2649_22555297_1_1_1_1_1,00.html>.

Phishing (http://en.wikipedia.org/wiki/Phishing) is a more recent evolution of spam and represents a growing concern in the world of consumer safety. In this version, recipients receive spam which is disguised as legitimate mail from a known institution such as a bank. These mails often contain links to false websites which are used to gather sensitive user information.

Spam is popular for commercial purposes because it is an extremely cheap and effective way of reaching a large audience. E-mail addresses for mass-mailings are usually collected using web bots (http://en.wikipedia.org/wiki/Internet_bot) which search the Internet and harvest addresses from various websites.

Ethical considerations

- Spam often includes false or fraudulent information. Because the sender remains anonymous, it is currently not possible to prosecute for false claims.
- Spammers often prey on the goodwill of recipients in order to gather mail addresses for their databases. For example, mails may be sent requesting recipients to add their personal information to a list in order to support a petition or cause. Often citing a cause such as a sick child requiring surgery, it falsely claims that a company or organisation has promised that money will be paid each time it is forwarded.
- Spam may contain malware (http://en.wikipedia.org/wiki/Malware).
- Another type of online fraud is “419” named after a Nigerian law prohibiting this type of victimisation. This typically involves promises of a share of a large sum of money in return for help with bank transfers.

- Spam can also be used as sabotage. One example is the bombardment and subsequent overloading of discussion groups with false messages.

Best practice

- Maintain a healthy scepticism about e-mails you receive. Do not open e-mails if you do not trust the source.
- Be especially wary of attachments. If you receive something that looks suspicious, or that you have not requested, delete it immediately without opening it.
- Check all links in e-mails before clicking on them. This can be done by holding your cursor over the link – the URL should appear in the bottom left-hand corner of your screen just above the task bar. If you are suspicious that a link does not lead to where it claims, type it into your browser instead of clicking on it.
- Use spam filters to avoid wasting time deleting unwanted mails: http://spam-filter-review.toptenreviews.com/).
- Avoid distributing your e-mail address on a large scale. Bear in mind that if you include your e-mail address on a website, web crawlers can pick it up and add it to distribution lists for spam.
- If you do need to post your e-mail address, you can disguise it by adding characters which will fool a web bot. See Lancaster University's tips on reducing your visibility at <http://www.lancs.ac.uk/iss/email/spam.htm#reduce>.
- Do not respond to spam. This will confirm your e-mail address to the spammer. Be aware that links promising to remove you from their mailing list may not be genuine. Automatic out-of-office replies also pose a problem since they send responses to spammers as well as legitimate contacts.

For further information

- European Union's anti-spam initiative: <http://europa.eu.int/information_society/topics/ecomm/index_en.htm>.
- The European Coalition Against Unsolicited Commercial E-mail: <http://www.euro.cauce.org/en/index.html>.
- Microsoft spam and phishing page. Bill Gates article of 28 June 2004 on "Preserving and enhancing the benefits of e-mail": <http://www.microsoft.com/mscorp/execmail/2004>.
- "419 Coalition fights 419 on the Internet": <http://home.rica.net/alphae/419coal/>.
- OECD on spam:<http://www.oecd.org/department/0,2688,en_2649_22555297_1_1_1_1_1,00.html>.

- Truth or Fiction is a website for Internet users to check up on claims made by commonly forwarded e-mails: <http://www.truthorfiction.com/>.
- Anti-spam tips: < http://www.anti-spam-tips.com/>.
- Help with spam: <http://www.spamhelp.org/>.
- SpamBayes, free spam filter which can plug into Outlook: <http://spambayes.sourceforge.net/>.
- Spam filter reviews: < http://spam-filter-review.toptenreviews.com/>.
- BBC Article (1 February 2005): "Junk e-mails on relentless rise": <http://news.bbc.co.uk/1/hi/technology/4225935.stm>.
- Radicata-Mirapoint study on e-mail bad habits: <http://www.messagingpipeline.com/news/159903196>.

Fact Sheet 7

Chat

What is chat?

Chat is a generic term that refers to interactive communication which takes place on a dedicated discussion channel. Users can talk to groups of people in chatrooms (http://en.wikipedia.org/wiki/Chatroom) or hold private conversations with selected friends by using instant messaging services (http://en.wikipedia.org/wiki/Instant_messaging).

Chatting is a very informal means of communication similar to face-to-face conversations and occurs between two or more persons. Chat discussions are usually typed but can also include video or audio streaming (http://en.wikipedia.org/wiki/Streaming) through the use of headsets and webcams. This form of communication is instantaneous and therefore different from e-mail, which does not depend on the recipient being present at the same time as the sender.

Is chat dangerous?

There has been a lot of negative publicity in recent months about risks young people might encounter when using chatrooms. Due to several high-profile criminal cases, parents and teachers often worry about the possibility of children coming into contact with paedophiles in chatrooms. Although these dangers do exist, it is important to keep these fears in perspective. A vast majority of chatroom users are who they say they are, and most chat communication is completely innocent. Rather than preaching fear or banning the use of chat, adults should empower the young by teaching them how to stay safe. Some basic rules to follow are:

- Never give out your personal information or post photos of yourself.
- Always bring an adult with you if you are going to meet a chatroom friend.
- Tell an adult if anything you have encountered in a chat session makes you uncomfortable.

Educational applications of chat

Teachers often underestimate how important chat is to young people. Chat and instant messaging are popular pastimes and are transforming the way young people communicate with each other. It is entirely feasible to harness this force and apply it as an educational tool. Some ideas include:

- Brainstorming sessions and problem-centred real time discussions.
- Role-playing games and simulations.
- Exchange of opinions and debates and small-group panel discussions.
- Tutoring and guidance.
- Group investigation.
- Creation of an online community.

How to get started

There are many kinds of free chat programes available on the Web. You can find a wide range by searching for "chat" in any search engine (http://en.wikipedia.org/wiki/Search_engine). Many web-based chat programs such as Yahoo Chat at <http://chat.yahoo.com/?myHome>, ICQ at <http://www.icq.com/> and AOL Chat at <http://site.aol.com/community/ chat/allchats.html> provide a wide variety of chatrooms with real-time discussion groups. Users must often first download a small application to enable chat and register with the moderator but can then login and participate freely.

Instant messaging (http://en.wikipedia.org/wiki/Instant_message) applications, which allow private conversations with select users, now surpass chatrooms in popularity, see <http://www.saferinternet.org/ww/en/pub/insafe/news/articles/0305/uk_ukcgo.htm>. These capabilities can be found by searching for "instant messaging" in any search engine (http://en.wikipedia.org/wiki/Search_engine). Users download an application to enable instant messaging and then compile a list of people with whom they want to chat. Because communication takes place in a restricted user group, instant messaging is often considered "safer" than chatting in chatrooms.

How to use a chatroom

- Open your chat program.
- Provide a username and password if necessary.
- Choose an appropriate chatroom. Usually there are rooms for different purposes and topics, for example automotive interest groups, subject-specific study groups, chats for teachers and so forth.
- Once you are logged in, you will see the participants' conversation scrolling on the main text screen.
- Type your message and press "enter" or click "send" to post it so that chat participants can see it.
- If you want to send a message to one specific person, select a person from the participant list in the window.
- Many chatrooms can also be used for peer-to-peer file exchange: (http://en.wikipedia.org/wiki/Peer_to_peer). Chatrooms enable the swapping of files too large to be sent by e-mail (http://en.wikipedia.org/wiki/Email).

How to use instant messaging

- Open your instant messaging application (http://en.wikipedia.org/wiki/Instant_message).
- Check your list of contacts to find out who is online and available to chat.
- You can add new contacts by entering in their e-mail address (http://en.wikipedia. org/wiki/Email) and inviting them to join your contact group. They will receive an e-mail invitation and if they agree, they will be registered in your list. This will enable you to chat with them real-time when you are both online.
- Click on that person's ID to send a message and open a dialogue for communication.
- Type your message and press "enter" or click "send" to post it so that chat participants can see it.

About ethics

Chat is text-based. Because social cues, gestures and non-verbal communication cannot be transmitted while typing, misunderstandings can easily occur online. One should be as agreeable, polite and well-mannered as in real-life situations and make a habit of using good netiquette (http://en.wikipedia.org/wiki/Netiquette). Humour and emotions can also be shown through use of emoticons (http://en.wikipedia.org/wiki/Emoticons), small symbols that look like faces written sideways.

When chatting with strangers on the Web, one should also remember that it is always possible that people may not be who or what they say they are. Closed groupware (http://en. wikipedia.org/wiki/ Groupware) chats which provide conferencing possibilities for use in a school or classroom setting are safer to use and do not have this problem because participants represent a limited user group. See <http://www.netlingo. com/right.cfm?term=username>.

It is important to remember that file exchange between users is vulnerable to security. Make sure that all files have been scanned for viruses before sharing them and scan anything you receive before opening it (see Fact Sheet 16 on security).

Some rules of thumb

The language used in chatting is fragmented, associative and very colloquial; a chat participant must not only be fast but flexible enough to switch from one topic and even one discussion to another. The supporting role of the teacher is very important when assuring quality of content and balanced participation by all those who contribute to the chat. The younger students are, the more important it is that the chat is hosted and moderated by the teacher.

- Follow the discussion actively during the whole chat session.
- Agree on the schedule of the session beforehand: everyone should be present at the same time.

- Be polite and kind, as if you were face-to-face.
- Remember that a carelessly written message can hurt even if this was not your intention.
- A short message works best. Do not monopolise a real-time chat session by pasting chunks of pre-written text which the others are obliged to read and respond to.
- Chat style is close to a stream of consciousness style. Try to read carefully others' messages and understand what they are trying to say. This may involve filling in the blanks.
- Remember not to share your username and password.

Some ideas for classroom work

- Pick a topic and have students ask each other questions and exchange information in a chat setting.
- Decide on a study topic, such as poetry in 19th-century England. Gather some orientation material to help students to do their pre-lesson activities. Have the students work on their assignments in pairs or small groups. This working phase should be organised along the lines of a group study model. (Chat works at its best in small-group interactions, that is 2-6 students).
- At the end of the project, students prepare presentations suitable for a chat session. Chat starts with small-group presentations of different study topics. The study community sums up together what they have learned during the course.
- Because chat sessions model real-life conversations, they offer students opportunities for authentic interaction and are therefore useful in studying foreign languages. The teacher can encourage students to participate in the discussion, advising them to post short messages. Interaction can be enhanced by creating roles for students: one may be an innovator, another a critic. The other students can follow the discussions at first and later provide feedback.
- Environment Online (ENO) at <http://eno.joensuu.fi/tools/chat.htm> is an international web-based environmental education project. At the beginning of the course, students get their topics from the web pages of the project. The students collect scientific and empirical environmental data, measure different phenomena or take photographs.
- During each theme period, virtual lessons are arranged in the form of interactive and synchronous real-time chats <http://www.netlingo.com/right.cfm?term=real%20time% 20chat>, electronic questionnaires and message boards (http://en.wikipedia.org/wiki/ Message_boards). Before and after lesson activities, students share ideas and monitor their tasks via chat and reflect on what they have learned.

For further information

- Elementary School Educators' Chat: <http://k6educators.about.com/mpchat.htm>.
- Teachers Net Chatroom: < http://teachers.net/chatrooms/>.
- Voila Chat (in French): < http://chat.voila.fr/>.
- International Review of Research in Open and Distance Learning: The Development of Social Climate in Virtual Learning Discussions: <http://www.irrodl.org/content/v3.1/mioduser.html>.
- Student Chatrooms (United Kingdom): <http://www.ukstudentchat.com/>.
- In-room chat as a social tool: <http://www.openp2p.com/lpt/a/3071>.
- The Meaning of Chat – a hyper dictionary: <http://www.hyperdictionary.com/computing/chat>.
- See Wikipedia at for a list of basic emoticons: (http://en.wikipedia.org/wiki/Emoticon#Basic_examples).
- Instant messaging: Friend or Foe of student writing? A graduate student in Educational Technology discusses the impact of "speak" on student writing: <http://www.newhorizons.org/strategies/literacy/oconnor.htm>.

Fact Sheet 8

Newsgroups

Introduction

A newsgroup is a discussion group with a focus on a particular topic. They date back to the early days of the Internet and even predate the World Wide Web (WWW).

Each newsgroup consists of a collection of communication in the form of electronic mail messages. There are hundreds of thousands of newsgroups worldwide and the more active groups receive hundreds of new messages each day. The messages are divided into threads, which record and display the sender's name and the time the message was sent.

They are still used extensively, and most servers and browsers today make them available to interested users.

Education

- Newsgroups are a useful resource for finding out information.
- Newsgroups can provide a fertile forum for discussions, thereby sharpening students' debating skills.
- Teachers can share information and experiences about a subject or teaching methodology.

Ethical considerations and risks

- Very few newsgroups are fully moderated and users are not tracked. This can be exploited for illegal activities such as distribution of copyrighted material or child pornography.
- Newsgroups have their own social conventions called "netiquette" (http://en.wikipedia. org/wiki/Netiquette).
- Some newsgroup users abusing their anonymity post critical messages and exhibit anti-social behaviour such as flaming (http://en.wikipedia.org/wiki/Flaming).

How to

- Usenet (http://en.wikipedia.org/wiki/Usenet) is the network which supports newsgroups. Your Internet service provider (ISP) decides which ones to offer (http://en.wikipedia.org/wiki/ Internet_service_provider). It is also possible to find public servers which will allow access.

- You can access many newsgroups using a news client. This is included in some mail programs such as Outlook Express. See <http://www.microsoft.com/windows/ie/using/howto/oe/gettingnews.mspx> for information on how to do this, with or without Outlook Express.
- Newsgroups already cover a range of specialised topics, but you can create your own newsgroup. This is a tricky process however. The "Big 8" categories (the original 8 newsgroups) have a slow and democratic process for accepting new groups. You should post your suggestion to news.groups.
- The more anarchic "alt" (http://en.wikipedia.org/wiki/Alt_hierarchy) newsgroups are outside the Big 8. You can post your idea for a new alt group in the alt.config newsgroup.

Best practice

- Be wary of publishing your e-mail address. You may get unwanted mail either from other newsgroup users or from junk mail spammers picking it up with web bots (see Fact Sheet 6 on spam).
- When first joining a newsgroup be sure to check the frequently asked questions (FAQ) (http://en.wikipedia.org/wiki/Faq) for guidelines. This will give you an idea of the netiquette of the newsgroup. Different newsgroups have different rules.
- Keep your messages as short as possible but make sure you give all relevant information. For example, if seeking the answer to a technical problem, give precise details about the hardware and software you are using.

For further information

- Google newsgroups at <http://groups.google.com/> has a complete list of newsgroups and an archive of over 1 billion postings.
- Dartmouth college tips on online classroom discussions: <http://www.dartmouth.edu/~webteach/articles/discussion.html>.
- Advice on creating a Big 8 newsgroup by David Lawrence and Russ Allbery: <http://www.faqs.org/faqs/usenet/creating-newsgroups/part1/>.
- Wikipedia entry for newsgroups: (http://en.wikipedia.org/wiki/Newsgroups).
- Newzbot has a number Usenet resources, including a search for public servers hosting newsgroups: <http://www.newzbot.com/>.

Fact Sheet 9

World-wide libraries

What is the difference between an online and a digital library?

The original idea behind the creation of the Internet was to develop an electronic library for the easy access and distribution of information: see <http://www.living internet.com/i/ ii_summary.htm>. In many ways this goal has been accomplished: today the Internet functions as an enormous library. More than 18 000 libraries are now present on the Internet and have a web page at <http://www.libdex.com/>.

A distinction should be made between libraries with a presence on the Web, and digital or electronic libraries. Online libraries maintain a simple web page providing users with basic information on programmes, activities, collections and contact details. They may include the lending of physical books listed in catalogues and which can be ordered over the Internet. Universities and other learning institution libraries often provide such services, though many public libraries offer them on the Internet too. Digital libraries offer the service of accessing books online, usually digitised as html script (http://en.wikipedia.org/ wiki/Html), meaning it looks like a web page, or as plain text (ASCII) (http://en.wikipedia.org/wiki/ASCII) documents, or as MSWord or Adobe PDF documents at <http://www.census.gov/main/www/pdf.html>.

Why use online libraries at school?

- The research skills necessary to navigate both traditional and online libraries are similar. It is crucial to practise and hone these skills in all areas of the curriculum.
- There are thousands of category-specific libraries on the Web at <http://dir.yahoo. com/Reference/Libraries/> that relate specifically to curriculum areas and themes. A webquest is "an inquiry-oriented activity in which some or all of the information that learners interact with comes from resources on the Internet". The model at <http://webquest.org/> can be very useful when creating activities for classroom participants to use library facilities on the Internet while developing a range of core skills, such as research, archiving, literacy, analysis and evaluation.

Ethical issues

- Individuals and institutions need to apply the safety criteria listed in Fact Sheets 15, 16 and 18 on privacy, security and shopping online respectively, and the evaluation criteria in Fact Sheet 3 on searching for information. Libraries may require a subscription fee or registration in order to use the facilities.

- Subscription libraries: These libraries typically require an annual fee, and may require membership of a university or institution.
- Free libraries are restricted to publishing materials which do not have copyright restrictions. The original trendsetter is the Gutenberg Project: <http://promo.net/pg/>.
- Registration libraries require a simple registration of your details in order to access their materials. Be sure to check the privacy policy and the conditions of use: <http://www.netlingo.com/right.cfm?term=privacy%20policy>.
- Most libraries will provide access according to certain rules. These rules at <http://www.gallowglass.org/jadwiga/SCA/libraries.html#Copyright__Plagiarism> will require at least that the user honours the copyright criteria of the material. Remember that unless the materials are in the public domain, you may not redistribute or publish materials without the permission of the publisher.
- Copyright is also a personal responsibility. The most common temptation is plagiarism, which is the use of someone else's work without crediting the source. Be sure to credit your sources, and instil the habit among your students.

Ideas for classroom work

- Identify the public libraries in your country that are on the Internet at <http://dspace.dial.pipex.com/town/square/ac940/eurolib.htm>. Ask your class to order a book from one of these libraries to support a current research activity.
- Using a current theme in your classroom, identify a category library at <http://vlib.org/>. Consider building a webquest around resources from this library, or use an existing webquest at <http://sesd.sk.ca/teacherresource/webquest/webquest.htm>. You can find webquests by using a search engine (http://en.wikipedia.org/wiki/Search_engine).
- Using the same theme, identify a text in the public domain (http://promo.net/pg/) and proof read or translate this text as part of the voluntary online projects to publish texts online.
- Consider creating an electronic library at school. This could start with one book turned into a web page or ASCII text, and stored on your school server. The International Association of School Librarianship (IASL), <http://www.iasl-slo.org/>, provides related policy information at <http://www.iasl-slo.org/documents3.html> and guidelines.

Best practice

- Before encouraging students to use online libraries, make sure to review basic library skills and research strategies: <http://www.acts.twu.ca/lbr/preface.htm>.

- Before requiring students to download files, talk to your school's network administrator. You should check to make sure there is space on the school server for downloading (http://www.walthowe.com/glossary/d.html#download) and storing files and archiving (http://en.wikipedia.org/wiki/Archiving#Computing_sense) them appropriately.
- Make sure that the online library usage tasks you set are possible. Check that the resources exist, and that the URL (http://en.wikipedia.org/wiki/URL) addresses work.
- Many files that you will download will be in Adobe PDF format to protect copyright. Make sure that you have downloaded and installed a recent version of the Acrobat reader in order to ensure that students can open these files. This can be done from <http://www.adobe.com/products/acrobat/readstep2.html>.
- The basic safety principles you apply when using the Internet should be applied when using online libraries. Check privacy statements, conditions of usage and scan files for viruses.

For further information

- The World e-book Foundation offers thousands of texts: <http://www.netlibrary.net/>.
- The Library Spot provides a free virtual library resource centre: <http://www.libraryspot.com/>.
- The International Association of School Librarians provides a storehouse of information, assistance, professional development and guidance specifically for school libraries: <http://www.iasl-slo.org/>.
- The Alex Catalogue of Electronic Texts is a collection of public domain documents from American and English literature as well as Western philosophy: <http://www.infomotions.com/alex2/>.
- The Electronic Text Centre collection of the library of the University of Virginia, where you can browse in 15 languages: <http://etext.lib.virginia.edu/uvaonline.html>.
- Research Strategies: Finding Your Way through the Information Fog: <http://www.acts.twu.ca/lbr/textbook.htm>.
- List of 1 000 + webquests from Saskatoon School Division Teaching Resources: <http://sesd.sk.ca/teacherresource/webquest/webquest.htm>.
- Article "Historical Research in the Modern Library": <http://www.gallowglass.org/jadwiga/SCA/libraries.html>.

Fact Sheet 10

Music and images on the Internet

Introduction

The Internet, as a multimedia platform, offers a large number of modes of communication including audio files, video files and digital photographs. These resources have a great impact since they go beyond linguistic, cultural and national barriers.

The major legal issues are copyright infringement and illegal content.

Copyright

- A number of international laws and agreements are in place. In 1996 more than 100 countries signed two World Intellectual Property Organisation (WIPO) treaties, which address digital content: <http://www.wipo.int/treaties/en/>.
- A creator of audio-visual material automatically has copyright unless he or she waives it.
- Most countries' laws maintain copyright 50-70 years after the creator's death.
- There is usually more than one copyright holder of a piece of music. Author, performing artist, record company and publisher may all own rights or "related rights".
- Aside from the economic aspect, a creator of audio-visual content has "moral rights" (http://en.wikipedia.org/wiki/Moral_rights). This relates to the right to be recognised as the creator and the right for the work not to be altered or edited without permission.
- Music and films can be bought online (see Fact Sheet 18 on online shopping). There are several sites for purchasing music online, such as iTunes at <http://www.apple. com/itunes/> and Napster at <http://www.napster.com/>, but similar services for online movies are in their infancy. Film downloads are becoming commonplace as more people have faster connections to download the large files involved.
- Buying music or films online usually gives limited or no right to copy or distribute them. For example, Apple's online music store iTunes allows a purchased track of music to be authorised on up to five computers within a household: <http://www.apple. com/itunes/share/>.

- The music industry has brought legal proceedings against both peer-to-peer software companies and individual filesharers. An uploader – someone who makes files available – is more likely to be prosecuted than a downloader.
- Creative commons at <http://creativecommons.org/> is a non-profit organisation offering an alternative to full copyright.

Illegal content

- The definition of illegal content varies from country to country.
- Illegal content most commonly refers to child pornography, extreme violence, political extremism or incitement to hatred against minority groups.
- Many countries have a hotline for reporting illegal content: <http://www.inhope.org/en/index.html>.
- Taking action may be difficult or slow depending on the nature of the content and where it is hosted.
- Hotlines work together with Internet service providers (ISPs) and the police, and are best-placed to tackle illegal content.
- Inhope is a network of national hotlines.

Ethical considerations and risks

- Worldwide global record sales decreased by 25% between 2001 and 2005. Many have attributed this to the rise of illegal music downloads.
- The music industry has responded by filing a number of lawsuits against websites and individual users.
- Using peer-to-peer software (http://en.wikipedia.org/wiki/Peer-to-peer) can be a security risk to your computer, as viruses (http://en.wikipedia.org/wiki/Viruses) and spyware (http://en.wikipedia.org/wiki/Spyware) are often distributed by attaching them to music and image files.

Education

- Educational establishments are, in certain cases, allowed to reproduce works and communicate them to the public. Refer to your national legislation or to the Directive 2001/29/EEC of 22 May 2001.
- Works used must be solely for teaching or scientific research purposes.
- Source, including the author's name should be indicated – except where this is impossible.
- No direct or indirect economic or commercial advantage must be gained from the use of this content.
- You need written permission from a parent or guardian before publishing photos of students online.
- In the case of content published on the school's website, all content, including content originating from children, is under the authority of the school.

In the classroom

- Have a discussion on moral aspects. Is piracy of audio-visual material stealing?
- Inform students about the risks of viruses and spyware from downloads.
- Inform students about the possibility of fines for downloading copyrighted music and film.
- Discuss harmful and illegal content. Surveys show many students deliberately or accidentally find this type of content on the Internet, but few tell an adult.

Best practice

- Schools and companies should have an acceptable use policy (AUP), which includes issues on copyright and illegal material.
- Parents should agree certain rules on Internet use with children.

Copyright

- Get written permission from a copyright holder before using material.
- Credit the author/creator of any material you use.
- Apply Creative Commons classifications to material you create to clarify how others may use it: <http://creativecommons.org/>.

Illegal content

- Software filters can help block some illegal websites.
- No filter is perfect. It is also important to discuss children's use of the Internet.
- Encourage children to talk about their online experiences.
- Report illegal content to a hotline, see inhope below.

For further information

- World Intellectual Property Organisation (WIPO): <http://www.wipo.int>.
- Pro-music is a good source of information on online music piracy. It has a leaflet for kids and a Q & A on music downloads: <http://www.pro-music.org/copyright/faq.htm>.
- Inhope is the network of hotlines for reporting illegal content on the Internet: <http://www.inhope.org/>.
- The Council of Europe media page has information on its work in the field of copyright: <http://www.coe.int/T/E/human_rights/media/>.
- European Commission information on intellectual property rights: <http://www.europa.eu.int/comm/internal_market/copyright/index_en.htm>.

- Information on EU legislation in the field of intellectual property: <http://www.europa.eu.int/scadplus/leg/en/s06020.htm>.
- The International Federation for the Phonographic Industry (IFPI) gives a legal overview about online music: <http://www.ifpi.org/>.
- BBC article, "European Commission plans for EU-wide copyright": <http://news.bbc.co.uk/1/hi/technology/4663731.stm>.

Fact Sheet 11

Creativity

How does the Internet promote creativity?

Because of the flexible nature of the Internet, today's classroom setting is less rigid than ever before. Rapidly evolving technology provides students ample opportunity to explore topics that interest them and to learn in non-traditional ways.

Using the tools that modern technology provides, students can create professional-standard material that can be published for audiences anywhere in the world. They can conduct experiments and simulations of all kinds within the classroom, or interactively with other learners across the Internet.

The Internet has globalised education and provides the opportunity for students to reach out in real-time to peers all over the globe.

Enhancing creative processes in learning

- Successful technology integration in the classroom offers students a chance to show their innovation, individuality and creativity.
- The use of creativity software and the Internet enables you to improve learning in your classroom in meaningful ways.
- The possibility to express creativity and take on a more active role in the classroom encourages learning and growth.
- Students can use the Internet to contact artists anywhere in the world to ask for advice and opinions on their work. Artists can use chat (see Fact Sheet 7), video conferencing, see <http://www.netlingo.com/right.cfm?term=video%20 conferencing> or virtual meetings to give workshops.
- Using Internet message boards (http://en.wikipedia.org/wiki/Message_boards), students can work together, collaborating online on shared projects. This provides a new creative outlet and the brainstorming involved can stimulate the creative process.

How can we ensure that creativity is not inhibited?

There are several issues to be taken into consideration in the learning environment.

- Access issues: Does everyone in your school have access to necessary equipment? Do all students have the same access opportunities?

- Equality: All students – boys and girls the world over regardless of age or ability – should benefit from equal opportunities to be creative, that is to know how to use and create with all available technology.
- The online safety factor: Do the filters (http://en.wikipedia.org/wiki/Internet_filter) put in place to keep students safe also inhibit access to material needed? How can this be dealt with so that students can enjoy safe access to information they need? (See Fact Sheet 14 on labelling and filtering.)
- Training for teachers: In many classrooms students are more Internet savvy than their teachers. Teachers need to benefit from all training opportunities available to them in order to properly guide their students in all aspects of ICT.
- Technical support issues: Does your school provide the technical support needed so that programmes and projects are not inhibited?
- A buffered environment: Creativity allows expression of your feelings as an individual. Although you should ideally limit constraints on a student's creative processes, it is important to retain control over the output, especially if brainstorming occurs in a group setting, such as chat. A teacher or other authority figure should be present to guide the work in a constructive manner.

Boosting creativity in the classroom

- A webquest, <http://webquest.sdsu.edu/materials>, is an inquiry-based approach to integrating the Internet into the classroom. Additional webquest resources are available from the Canadian SESD teaching resources website: <http://sesd.sk.ca/teacherresource/webquest/webquest.htm>.
- Students can challenge their creativity by building their own websites. This stimulates creative thought processes in different ways by requiring input on graphics and content.
- Students can collaborate on projects that develop writing skills by producing online books and stories.
- Hot Potatoes software at <http://hotpot.uvic.ca/> is free of charge and can be used to create interactive quizzes and activities for the Web.
- Students can create interactive stories with multiple outcomes with software such as that available at Quia's website: <http://www.quia.com/>.
- Secondary school and university students can create their own 3D learning environment at <http://www.activeworlds.com/> with software like Active Worlds. They can build their ideal landscape, their own virtual campus. They can also collaborate with other students in projects on different topics.

Best practice

- The Internet can be used as a basic research tool for background information on different topics. Students can then apply the knowledge they have gained to an assignment that stimulates creativity. Technology provides students the opportunity and the freedom to develop higher-order thinking.
- The Internet and other modern technology allows for powerful communication and collaboration between students of different countries and cultures. More

than ever before, students have the possibility to brainstorm creative solutions with a broad peer base.

- Teachers have found that implementing technology in the classroom in such a way as to provide hands-on activities allows students opportunities for problem-solving and innovation.
- Keep learning goals in mind: the key to reaching these goals is to focus on the process taken to get to the product rather than on the product itself.
- When students publish the results of creative activities online, they need to respect copyright (http://en.wikipedia.org/wiki/Copyright). Remind them to cite their sources when using material created by others.

For further information

A number of websites can be used as a starting point to involve students in projects where creativity is encouraged and collaboration is essential.

- ThinkQuest is an international competition which challenges students and teachers to create websites on educational topics: <http://www.thinkquest.org/>.
- Global Schoolhouse Cyberfair is an online meeting place where parents, students and educators can collaborate, interact, develop, publish and discover learning resources: <http://www.globalschoolnet.org/GSH/>.
- Future Problem Solvers Program: Engages students in creative problem solving by simulating critical and creative thinking skills: <http://www.fpsp.org/>.
- Mr Coulter's Internet tendency: to infinity and beyond. An experienced elementary school teacher uses online publishing to motivate young writers: <http://www.newhorizons.org/strategies/literacy/coulter.htm>.
- Online Fanfiction: What technology and popular culture can teach us about writing and literacy instruction can be found at <http://www.newhorizons.org/strategies/literacy/black.htm>. A doctoral candidate at the University of Wisconsin explores an alternate literary world in cyberspace, which is often a compelling avenue for creative writing outside the classroom.
- Gateway to educational materials provides educators with quick and easy access to educational resources. Do a search for "creativity" for lesson plans, classroom ideas: <http://www.thegateway.org/>.
- Webquest reading and training materials: <http://webquest.sdsu.edu/materials.htm>.
- List of 1 000+ webquests from SESD: <http://sesd.sk.ca/teacherresource/webquest/webquest.htm>.

Fact Sheet 12

Games

Introduction

Over half of all children who use the Internet play online games: 70% in the United Kingdom and 90% in Scandinavian countries, according to a 2003 SAFT (safety, awareness, facts, tools) survey at <http://www.saftonline.org/>.

There are many different game genres such as arcade, role-playing, strategy and sports games. They can be played alone or with partners, in closed circles or even with thousands of strangers playing together.

Investment in game development has increased rapidly in recent years. In 2005, the average cost of making a game was $5-7 million, with some titles costing over $20 million to develop.

A report by DFC Intelligence at <http://www.dfcint.com/> forecasts that global video game sales will reach $26 billion in 2010.

Personal development and educational value

- Game-playing is more than entertainment: it is an enriching collaborative activity enjoyed by children and adults of all ages.
- Games foster creativity and interaction and play an important role in social and intellectual development.
- Games represent one of the rare occasions when adults and children can exchange ideas on an equal footing (inter-generational communication).
- Children learn about democracy by playing within different social structures, in an environment bordered by rules and parameters.
- Games often involve sharing and respecting the rights and property of others, sometimes even bringing players into contact with other cultures and intercultural practices. Children can practise social skills without fear of failure and with a sense of control.
- Because games require children to obey rules and follow directions, they increase their capacity for self-discipline and autonomy.
- Puzzles, board games, adventures and quests offer opportunities for players to develop strategic thinking and problem-solving skills.
- Other games can be used to increase fine motor and spatial skills in younger children and for therapeutic purposes with the physically disabled.

- Online games are useful for introducing newcomers to technology and generally fostering interest in ICT (http://en.wikipedia.org/wiki/Information_technology).
- Games can be integrated into almost any area of the curriculum, from mathematics to social studies and languages.

Potential risks

- The violent nature of some computer games has been loosely associated with violent behaviour in young people. However a Danish Media Council report in 2002 suggested that the violent aspects of some games were not more influential than TV or film violence: <http://resources.eun.org/insafe/datorspel_Playing_with.pdf>.
- Studies attempting to determine the proportion of young people affected by computer game addiction have had widely different results. This is because there is currently no agreement on an objective way to decide at what stage heavy use of computer games can be considered excessive or addictive. Gamers may play a high number of hours per week without adverse effects to their social and professional lives. However, it is generally accepted that addiction is a problem among a small proportion of gamers. This problem was highlighted when the case of a Korean man who died after a 50-hour game session was widely reported in the media in August 2005.
- Some games have been accused of supporting racial or gender stereotyping.
- Some online games allow the possibility to meet and communicate with strangers.

Best practice

- Labeling and rating systems encourage games industry actors to act responsibly by requiring them to define and describe their products. This also helps game buyers judge the content and age suitability of games and to navigate the game market more safely.
- Monitor the number of hours spent playing. Take action if other social activities are avoided or children and young people skip school in order to spend time gaming.
- Gaming communities can foster a sense of belonging and can lead children to trust too readily. Remind them that online friends may not always be who they say they are. It is important not to give out personal information to anyone online.

For further information

- Entertainment and Leisure Software Publishers Association (ELSPA): <http://www.elspa.com/>.
- Game Studies: International journal of computer game research: <http://www.gamestudies.org/>.
- See charts of top-selling games, and games news, descriptions, research reports and legislation reviews on the Elspa site: <http://www.elspa.com/>.
- The Pan European Games Information (PEGI) website contains rating and labelling information: <http://www.pegi.info/pegi/index.do>.
- "Parents ignore game ratings" – BBC article, June 2005: <http://news.bbc.co.uk/1/hi/technology/4118270.stm>.
- Online games can be found at Amic Games at <http://www.amicgames.com/> and Yahoo! Games at <http://dir.yahoo.com/Recreation/Games/>.
- "Playing with fire: how do computer games affect the player", Danish Council report: <http://resources.eun.org/insafe/datorspel_Playing_with.pdf>.

Fact Sheet 13

Distance learning

What is distance learning?

Distance learning (http://en.wikipedia.org/wiki/Distance_learning) is defined by Wikipedia (see also http://en.wikipedia.org/wiki/Main_Page) as "a method of teaching in which the students are not required to be physically present at a specific location during the term". This method opens up lifelong learning opportunities to students of all countries and all ages, making it possible for them to earn diplomas, certificates and degrees from almost any online university in the world.

Distance learning began with generations of adults seeking advanced education at home, in the military or on the job. Courses used to be done by correspondence, with material sent back and forth through the traditional postal system. These days, however, distance learning has evolved to take advantage of current technology. It thrives via the Internet, and students can study for degrees without ever setting foot in a brick-and-mortar classroom. Advances in distance learning have revolutionised the arena of advanced education. For example:

- Lectures can be given via streaming media (http://en.wikipedia.org/wiki/Streaming_ media) or as printed material saved in files which are stored on the educator's server (http://en.wikipedia.org/wiki/Web_server).
- Students communicate with the teacher and each other through message boards (http://en.wikipedia.org/wiki/Message_boards), e-mail (http://en.wikipedia.org/wiki/E-mail) and chat (http://en.wikipedia.org/wiki/Chat).
- Assignments are uploaded into a drop box and even quizzes and exams can be automated and taken online.
- Course materials are readily available and easily updated.
- The online format provides unparalleled flexibility for self-paced work.

What are the advantages of distance learning?

- The Internet is perfect for setting up a virtual learning environment. Students can, for example, stay in their own hometown while studying at a virtual university abroad.
- Providing students with an access to the whole base of learning material gives them the opportunity to become more autonomous in their learning process.
- Students have more ownership of their own learning, and the role of the teacher is transformed into the role of a coach.

- Courses are not restricted to the opening hours of "normal" schools or universities, so everyone can benefit from more opportunities to become lifelong learners.
- Distance learning changes the behaviour of both the teacher and the student. Successful students develop persistence and organisational skills and the teacher must become more conversant in technology.

Points to consider when choosing a distance-learning programme

You should be aware that you, as the user, are responsible for taking certain precautions when choosing a degree or other distance-learning programme.

- Remember that the Internet is not a regulated environment. There are dubious distance-learning institutions out there alongside the legitimate ones. Make sure you research a programme/organisation thoroughly before enrolling.
- Security issues are always key, as with any exchange of information over the Internet. Viruses (http://en.wikipedia.org/wiki/Virus) and hackers (http://en.wikipedia.org/wiki/Hacker) can wreak havoc on a distance-learning system so be sure to consult Fact Sheets 15 and 16 on privacy and security to see which precautions you should take.
- Copyright (http://en.wikipedia.org/wiki/Copyright) is usually protected by the law of the student's home country. However, when following distance-learning programmes in other countries be sure to check that the learning sources are covered by international copyright.
- Fair use and payment of courses is also a hot issue: students are expected to use learning facilities in a trustworthy way and to pay for their courses on time.

Best practice

The Internet is changing the way we learn and it is very important for students to have access to all information and tools available to help them learn. The "digital divide" (http://en.wikipedia.org/wiki/Digital_divide) is seen as a leading issue in the economic and social growth of many nations and the use of distance learning can narrow this gap.

Distance learning can increase student learning in measurable ways. It provides Internet training with hands-on experience for students, their families and teachers. Distance learning provides an opportunity for students to build new skills and qualifications and grow in new directions.

For further information

- The Distance Learning Network provides information about distance learning, reports on its effectiveness – advantages, disadvantages, and techniques: <http://www.distancelearningnet.com/>.
- The Distance Education and Training Council contains a number of reports on distance learning which are available for free download: <http://www.detc.org/otherdownld.html>.
- Yahoo! has a directory page for distance-learning programmes and institutions: <http://dir.yahoo.com/Education/Distance_Learning>.

Fact Sheet 14

Labelling and filtering

Labelling

Labelling refers to a quality-assurance tag or label displayed on software and websites, or integrated into the content of websites. It ensures that the product meets the criteria and standards designated by rating agencies such as Platform for Internet Content Selection (PICS) and the Internet Content Rating Association (ICRA).

Sites are labelled in order to protect minors, increase public trust and use of online transactions, and also to comply with legal standards. When labelling website content, a code is written into the webpage html, thereby detailing its contents so that the page can be rated. This rating – which is invisible on the page itself, details the nature of the content and is detected by filtering mechanisms, which will subsequently either block or load the page.

Websites can also be branded with "Quality Labels" and "Trustmarks", labels which signify that specific regulations have been met. These regulations often include prescriptions about secure transactions (see Fact Sheet 18 on shopping online). Two well-known quality labels include Verisign at <http://www.verisign.com/> and Trust-e at <http://www.truste.org/>.

Filtering

- Filtering is the process of detecting and blocking inappropriate content on the Internet. It can be done within browsers and proxies, or by installing software censors.
- An alternative to filtering is "white listing", whereby access is allowed only to certain pre-approved sites.

Education

- Filters can be valuable in reducing the risk of students accessing inappropriate or harmful material.
- The issues raised by labelling and filtering practices are rich in material for citizenship and/or social studies themes. Start a debate on the subject of online filtering. Is it an acceptable and necessary form of censorship?

Issues

- The labelling and rating of websites remains a largely voluntary practice, except where countries have laws to enforce certain standards.
- Currently only a small percentage of pages are labelled by the authors.
- Filtering software-services label pages according to their value systems and social agendas.
- Filters may block useful sites relating to contraception or sex education due to certain key words they contain.
- Some countries block sites of opposing political parties or ideologies.
- Some people consider filtering as a form of censorship and therefore against the spirit of the Internet. Others claim that if filter software did not exist, governments would be under pressure to regulate online content.

How to

- To label content you have created on a site of your own, follow instructions on a rating site such as ICRA at <http://www.icra.org/>.
- You will be asked to classify the material according to a number of set criteria.
- Most browsers can be set to filter out specific sites. For example, in Microsoft Explorer, this option can be found under "security options".
- Very few computers are sold with filter software pre-installed. You will need to purchase a dedicated filter program for a more sophisticated approach to filtering sites. A number of products are available on the market.
- Most filter programs will allow you to specify what types of content you wish to filter or allow.

Best practice

- Have a close look at how a filter works before you install it. Does it make any ideological or cultural decisions in its filtering that you do not agree with?
- Use electronic aids with discrimination, and do not believe the hype. Test product claims against personal experience.
- Talk to students, parents and staff about their usage and needs, and do so regularly. Creating an open discussion environment will do more to add value to your learners' Internet experience than censorship or witch-hunts.
- Consider "white listing" options – allowing access only to approved sites – for the youngest Internet users.
- Experts recommend that parents should take an interest in their children's online activities and spend time online together.
- Children and young people should be encouraged to talk about inappropriate material they find on the Internet. Report potentially illegal content to a hotline: <http://www.inhope.org>.

For further information

- The Internet Content Rating Association (ICRA) at <http://www.icra.org/> enables websites to apply labels according to different categories. It also offers its own free filter for download.
- The Platform for Internet Content Selection (PICS) at <http://www.w3.org/PICS/> is another system for applying labels to websites.
- Wikipedia entry on censorship in cyberspace: <http:/en.wikipedia.org/wiki/Censorship_in_cyberspace>.
- The Council of Europe media division website – information on their work promoting self-regulation and user empowerment: <http://www.coe.int/media>.
- NetNanny at <http://www.netnanny.com/> and Cyberpatrol at <http://www.cyberpatrol.com/> are among the well-known commercial filter products.
- ICRA at <http://www.icra.org/> and Weblocker at <http://weblocker.fameleads.com/> offer free filter software for download.
- Selfregulation.info provides in-depth reports from the University of Oxford's research project: <http://www.selfregulation.info/>.
- "A little less censorship" – BBC article: <http://news.bbc.co.uk/2/hi/technology/4080886.stm>.
- The OpenNet Initiative documents filtering and blocking worldwide: <http://www.opennetinitiative.net/>.
- The Electronic Frontier Foundation (EFF) aims to defend civil liberties on the Internet: <http://www.eff.org/>.
- The Censorware Project: <http://censorware.net/>.
- Internet Content Rating for Europe (INCORE) report – an executive summary of a report on self-labelling and filtering: <http://europa.eu/int/ISPO/iap/INCOREexec.html>.

Fact Sheet 15

Privacy

How private is the Internet?

- Privacy (http://en.wikipedia.org/wiki/Privacy) refers to the degree of control that a person has concerning access to and use of personal information.
- Most e-mail (http://en.wikipedia.org/wiki/E-mail) and Internet (http://en.wikipedia. org/wiki/Internet) users assume that personal information will not be used without permission and that information exchanges are private and secure. The reality, however, is very different.
- Every time you access a website or send e-mail, you leave information about yourself that could include your physical and computer address, telephone and credit card numbers, consumer pattern data and much more.
- Privacy is closely related to security; be sure to read thoroughly Fact Sheet 16 on security.

Why talk about privacy in class or at home?

- The technical and social aspects of privacy provide valuable learning themes. Technical aspects may be included in information technology (IT) studies, but should equally form part of a life-skills curriculum.
- Every student should have the skills necessary to negotiate the Internet safely, and that includes knowledge of self-protection, effective communication and responsibility toward others.
- There is a natural flow from this theme into the citizenship dimension of any curriculum. The issues raised about online privacy accurately mirror social issues predominant in most cultures today. Exploring the motivations of hackers (http://en.wikipedia.org/wiki/Hacker), crackers (http://en.wikipedia.org/wiki/Hacker#Hacker:_Intruder_and_ criminal) and privacy activists offers rich possibilities to discuss the value of democratic principles.

Ethical issues

- Online privacy is one of the most complex ethical and legal topics regarding the Internet.
- Everyone has a right to privacy and needs to be protected from malicious intent.

- We are accountable for all decisions we make about our own and others' rights, for example copyright (http://en.wikipedia.org/wiki/Copyright) and intellectual property (http://en.wikipedia.org/wiki/Intellectual_property).
- Freedom of speech is a politically accepted notion, however in practice this is a grey area with no easy answers. What is acceptable and what is not? How does one enforce the rules without encroaching on the rights of the speaker?

Ideas for classroom work

- Create a basic knowledge framework for privacy with your class. Define concepts, both technical and social, and identify prejudices and myths for discussion. Simply setting the questions "What is privacy?" and "Is privacy necessary?" should generate some strong views.
- Search for privacy sites on the Internet, and use traceroute (http://en.wikipedia.org/wiki/Traceroute) programs to locate the physical addresses of these sites to demonstrate the diverse geophysical issues governing legality on the Internet. Explore other issues (cultural, political and historical) that come up from the trace results. For example, choose a re-mailer (http://en.wikipedia.org/wiki/Remailer) site or anonymous proxy service, run a trace, then search for reasons why the services would be located in those countries.
- Explore the implications of privacy law, copyright and freedom of speech and information across national boundaries, or for different age and cultural groups.
- Teach students how to create secure passwords (http://en.wikipedia.org/wiki/Password#Factors_in_the_security_of_an_individual_password).

Best practice

- The golden rule: do not share your personal information with anyone you do not know and trust.
- Back up (http://en.wikipedia.org/wiki/Back_up) your system, and have a regular backup policy.
- Update security measures on your system and do some research on additional tools at <http://www.epic.org/privacy/tools.html> that will support your online preferences.
- Anti-virus (http://en.wikipedia.org/wiki/Antivirus) and firewall (http://en.wikipedia.org/wiki/Firewall_%28networking%29) software are an absolute necessity. You might also want to consider other tools such as pop-up blockers (http://en.wikipedia.org/wiki/Pop_up#Add-on_programs_that_block_pop-up_ads) and anti-spyware (http://en. wikipedia.org/wiki/Spyware). Be sure to check your system regularly.
- Use "strong passwords" (http://en.wikipedia.org/wiki/Password#Factors_in_the_security_of_an_individual_password) to protect your PC, e-mail and Internet connections.

- Before giving out private data, check for the locked padlock symbol that shows up in the toolbar. This is a sign that your transaction is taking place over a secure connection.

Cookies

- A cookie (http://en.wikipedia.org/wiki/HTTP_cookie) is a text file left on your computer when you visit a website. It cannot harm your computer, but will give access to information about your behaviour and interests. This can provide a more personal surfing atmosphere. For example, when registering with a website you may be greeted by name upon your return.
- It is important to decide how private you want to keep your online behavior. Since cookies can be used to track usage patterns and contact information they provide a possibility for encroachment on your privacy.
- You can use anti-spyware (http://en.wikipedia.org/wiki/Spyware) to help control the data your system is broadcasting and to clean out unwanted cookies.

Data protection

- Make sure your machine and e-mail programs are password protected (http://en.wikipedia.org/wiki/Password). Most home machines have "default" user and password settings which allow access through standard passwords like "test". See <http://www.netlingo.com/right.cfm?term=default>. Make sure you change these default settings to a more secure password and ID.
- It is best to encrypt (http://en.wikipedia.org/wiki/Encryption) any sensitive information which is sent over the Internet. Fortunately this is standard for most e-commerce (http://en.wikipedia.org/wiki/Ecommerce) transactions but you should still make sure that a page is secure before transmitting credit card information or bank account numbers.
- Different sections of your computer can be secured using passwords. Create passwords for folders containing valuable documents such as confidential projects, research, original designs and so forth.

For further information

- The Council of Europe's Legal Affairs page contains information about the work of the Council of Europe in the field of data protection: <http://www.coe.int/T/E/Legal_affairs/Legal_co-operation/Data_protection/>.
- The Electronic Privacy Information Center (EPIC) maintains a list of privacy tools and articles: <http://www.epic.org/privacy/tools.html>.
- Find out what your PC is telling anyone on the net who cares to look by using BrowserSpy: <http://gemal.dk/browserspy/>.

- Concerned about your civil liberties? These discussions on privacy could keep your citizenship class going for a while: Electronic Frontier Foundation at <http://www.eff.org/>, Privacy.org at <http://www.privacy.org/>, Privacy International at <http://www.privacyinternational.org/> and Privacy.net at <http://www.privacy.net/>.
- CyberAngels at <http://www.cyberangels.org/>, is an Internet security website with simple tutorials and explanations.
- TuCows at <http://www.tucows.com/>, is a website which provides access to over 40 000 shareware and freeware programs. It promises fast, local and safe virus and spyware free downloads.
- Zone Alarm at <http://www.zonelabs.com/store/content/home.jsp> is one of the better known firewall programs. It lets you set access controls for different programs which send information out over the Internet.
- CryptoHeaven is an encryption package which offers secure mail, file sharing and chat with symmetrical and asymmetrical encryption: <http://www.cryptoheaven.com/>.
- LavaSoft Ad-aware is an anti-trackware program that scans your computer and protects your privacy: <http://www.lavasoft.com/>.

Fact Sheet 16

Security

Introduction

- Your online security can be compared to security at home. You protect the contents by keeping the windows closed and the door locked.
- Malware (http://en.wikipedia.org/wiki/Malware) is a generic term for malicious software such as viruses (http://en.wikipedia.org/wiki/Computer_virus) that can infect a computer. Malware can have a number of effects, such as preventing the normal running of software or allowing unauthorised access or deletion of data.
- The most common forms of malware are viruses (http://en.wikipedia.org/wiki/Computer_virus) and worms (http://en.wikipedia.org/wiki/Computer_worm) which are self-replicating programs.
- Despite the name, not all viruses and other forms of malware are designed with malicious intent.
- An average of 10 new viruses are identified every day.
- Many of the issues relevant for security are also relevant for privacy (see Fact Sheet 15).

Education

- Discuss issues of self-protection and responsibility with students. Since many of the young are better-informed than adults, encourage them to share their knowledge and experience with each other and their families.
- A number of hackers and creators of viruses are among the youngest users of the Internet. Have a classroom discussion about these issues.

Ethical considerations and risks

- Your computer's security can have an effect on others. Viruses that infect your computer can be passed on to others.
- Anyone who stores personal data on clients or other acquaintances is responsible for keeping this information secure.
- Hacking (http://en.wikipedia.org/wiki/Hack_%28technology_slang%29) or other unauthorised access to information about others is a violation of others' rights.

- It is important to be cautious but do not go overboard with security measures! One of the Web's greatest qualities is its accessibility. Restricting rights or activating excessive filtering may constitute censorship or reduce accessibility.
- Spyware refers to programs which hijack a computer usually with commercial motives. This could involve adding unwanted advertising or stealing credit card information. Dialers are a form of spyware that cause modems to dial numbers without the user's authorisation. This has been used to make calls to premium rate phone lines.
- Cookies involve the storing of personal information. See Fact Sheet 15 on privacy for more details.

Best practice

- Install anti-virus software (http://en.wikipedia.org/wiki/Anti-virus_software) and keep it updated.
- Install security patches as soon as they are available. You can set some operating systems and programs to update automatically or inform you as soon as a patch is available for download.
- Install a firewall (http://en.wikipedia.org/wiki/Firewall_%28networking%29) to control traffic to and from your computer.
- Do not leave your computer unnecessarily connected to the Internet. Broadband subscriptions allow unlimited connection time but this can compromise security.
- Avoid using passwords (http://en.wikipedia.org/wiki/Password#Factors_in_the_security_of_an_individual_password) that have an obvious connection with you. Use a combination of letters and numbers.
- Set your browser (http://en.wikipedia.org/wiki/Web_browser) to "disable scripts". You can enable scripts for trusted sites.
- Do not open e-mails which may not be genuine (see Fact Sheet 5 on e-mail).
- Make sure you trust the source before downloading anything to your computer. Be particularly aware of peer-to-peer software (http://en.wikipedia.org/wiki/Peer_to_peer), which is notorious for aiding the distribution of spyware (see Fact Sheet 10 on music and images).
- Regularly back up important files to a location separate from your computer, such as on CD-Roms.
- If you are managing more than one user of a computer or network, make sure each user has appropriate rights. Restricting unnecessary user rights can help avoid accidental or deliberate security problems.
- Network administrators should create an AUP (http://en.wikipedia.org/wiki/AUP) so users do not jeopardise security of systems.
- The Windows operating system and Internet Explorer browser are the most common targets of malware. Consider alternatives such as open source software (http://en.wikipedia.org/wiki/Open_source) or Mozilla Firefox: <http://www.mozilla. org/>.

For further information

- Microsoft security page: <http://www.microsoft.com/security/default.mspx>.
- Apple security page: <http://www.apple.com/support/security/>.
- Detailed information for IT professionals: <http://www.searchsecurity.com>.
- European Network and Information Security Agency: <http://www.enisa.eu.int/>.
- OECD guidelines for the security of information systems and networks: <http://www.oecd.org/document/42/0,2340,en_2649_34255_15582250_1_1_1_1,00.html>.
- Information security magazine: <http://informationsecurity.techtarget.com/>.
- 2privacy.com's website has a privacy test for your computer: <http://www.2privacy.com/>.
- Online security advice from the governments of the UK at <http://www.itsafe.gov.uk/> and of the United States at <http://www.us-cert.gov/>.
- Information security guidelines for direct marketing: <http://www.the-dma.org/guidelines/informationsecurity.shtml>.

Fact Sheet 17

Bullying and harassment

What is the connection between the Internet and bullying or harassment?

Bullying (http://en.wikipedia.org/wiki/Bullying) and harassment (http://en.wikipedia.org/wiki/Harassment) have a huge impact on how people perceive themselves and the world around them.

The definition of bullying usually depends on who is defining it. However, for most people, bullying is an action which is taken against another person in order to cause harm, repeated in various forms over a period of time. Parents and children do not usually have the same perception of the scale of this problem.

Bullying can imply verbal or physical contact. These days, it can also include virtual bullying via the Internet, involving offensive or malicious e-mails, chat room or message board comments or, even more extreme, websites built with harmful intent towards an individual or certain groups of people.

Educators have always had to deal with bullying and harassment inside and outside of the classroom. It is imperative now for us to understand how this type of harassment involves the Internet as well.

How can bullying and harassment be dealt with at school or at home?

- If students are to learn productively, they need to be in an environment where they feel self-confident and safe.
- If a student is being harassed or bullied, then learning is restricted because he or she is unable to focus, feels threatened and loses self-confidence.
- It is the responsibility of teachers and parents to ensure the best learning environment possible, whether in the classroom, on the playground or working online.
- Students need to be able to take responsibility for their own actions, but bullying undermines confidence and self-esteem.
- Students who feel threatened (either online or off) need the help of a trusted adult. We should also remember that the person doing the bullying is also in need of guidance so that this behaviour is not repeated in the future.
- Schools should have specific guidelines in place as well. It would be a good idea to incorporate precautionary measures in your school's Internet policy to deal with bullying.

Ethical and safety issues

- Bullying and harassment in the classroom can lower the morale of the whole class, creating an atmosphere of fear and distrust and making learning nearly impossible.
- One preventive measure to help keep bullying or harassment from becoming a problem is to introduce anger management and conflict resolution into your curriculum. Well-chosen programes of this type will allow children and teenagers to discover their own talents as potential mediators in the conflicts. In this way, the risk of minor conflicts developing into threatening behaviour will be reduced both offline and online.
- Your school should have an explicit policy in place – commonly called an acceptable use policy (AUP) (http://en.wikipedia.org/wiki/Acceptable_Use_Policy) – to monitor when and how students and staff use the Internet at school. This document should explicitly explain that vulgar language and bullying / harassing language will not be tolerated. Direct consequences should be spelled out clearly for anyone who uses the Internet in an inappropriate manner.
- There should be a procedure in place that can document Internet usage, including who is online, when and where.
- Students should be told to discontinue contact with anyone who is harassing them or making them uncomfortable in any way when online.
- Students should immediately tell a trusted adult what has happened and, if possible, show them the offensive material. Then the adult should follow the procedures spelled out in the school's AUP.
- The procedure is the same as in real life, were a child to be harassed by someone. They should discontinue contact with the offender and tell a trusted adult about the incident. They should not feel as though they are alone or have to deal with it themselves.

In summary, school Internet use policy should include intervention methods such as conflict resolution, training of students and staff about what to do in the case of harassment online, provision of positive support to the targets of abuse and, wherever possible, help the abusers to change their behaviour. With such a policy in place, schools should have little problem dealing with bullying or harassment.

Ideas for classroom work

- Role play: students participate in a mock-conflict resolution process. The teacher assigns the roles and organises groups in which students are responsible for settling a dispute. The next step is to reverse the roles, allowing students to approach the issue from a different perspective.
- Discussion groups: students participate in discussion groups where their group work is evaluated, and where they are encouraged to talk about their impressions.

Best practice

Here are some ideas on how to handle online bullying, harassing e-mails or messages of any kind:

- Students should be instructed not to open e-mails from unknown sources.
- If an e-mail is opened and found to be offensive, delete it immediately.
- If a person keeps sending offensive or harassing e-mails and it is possible (by means of the e-mail address) to find out where the e-mail is being sent from, contact that service provider (http://en.wikipedia.org/wiki/Internet_Service_Provider) immediately to report the harassment.
- Your school's policy on bullying and/or acceptable user policy should have provisions on how to handle online harassment by students.
- Just as with any other kind of bullying, students should know they can come to you or another trusted adult anytime they are harassed online.

For further information

- Bullying.org: <http://www.bullying.org/>.
- Stop Bullying Now!: <http://www.stopbullyingnow.com/>.
- Know the risks: Challenging Cyber bullying: <http://www.media-awareness.ca/english/teachers/wa_teachers/safe_passage_teachers/risks_bullying.cfm>.
- What is cyber bullying?: <http://www.netalert.net.au/01569-what-is-cyber-bullying.asp?qid=10398>.
- Report bullying and harmful content to the Insafe network: <http://www.saferinternet.org/ww/en/pub/insafe/safety.htm>.

Fact Sheet 18

Shopping online

Introduction

E-commerce may be defined as the collection of services, software, and procedures that allows the sale of products online. Almost anything can be bought online from books to holidays, from clothing to electronics. Apart from material goods, you can also pay for services such as access to online content. According to Forrester Research at <http://www.forrester.com/my/1,,1-0,FF.html>, the European online retail market is expected to grow from € 40 billion in 2004 to € 167 billion by 2009.

Education

Young people need to be well-informed consumers. As online shopping gains in importance, it is vital that they understand how to take advantage of the benefits and avoid the risks associated with shopping online.

- Educate students to find out about the retailer and the conditions of sale.
- Invite students, alone or in groups, to look on specific commercial websites for products or services, with a particular goal in mind. For example, planning a holiday according to a fixed budget (see Fact Sheet 3 on searching for information).
- Plan an e-commerce website with your students (to sell school products, for instance), or do further work on existing initiatives of that kind already taken within the framework of the school. Study the structure of a good e-commerce website.

Ethical considerations and risks

- Protect your credit card data. Hackers can obtain credit card information by accessing your computer or by breaking into insecure websites holding your information.
- Criminals also obtain credit card or banking information by tricking people into giving them voluntarily. Phishing (http://en.wikipedia.org/wiki/Phishing) falls into this category. These attacks often target users of online shopping or payment sites, asking them to "reconfirm" details.
- Since online shopping often involves payment by credit card, consumers need to manage their finances carefully to avoid overspending.

Best practice

- Find out about the retailer or vendor. eBay, for example, allows vendors to build a reputation according to their track record and feedback. Do not buy from untrustworthy sources, especially those advertised by spam (see Fact Sheet 6).
- Make sure you are insured against fraudulent use of your credit cards. Check your statements carefully for any unauthorised purchases.
- Read the terms and conditions. The text may be long and technical but do not click to say you have read and understood it if you have not done so.
- Hidden costs. These may be taxes or delivery charges on the side of the seller. Customs duties may also be charged if you are ordering products from abroad.
- Is the site secure? A padlock or key symbol in the lower right-hand corner of the web browser will indicate secure pages. Look for Secure Sockets Layer (SSL) (http://en.wikipedia.org/wiki/Secure_Sockets_Layer) certificates which ensure that data is encrypted before it is sent.
- Make sure that you have control of your personal data. Pay attention to boxes relating to the retailer's options to retain your data or contact you for marketing purposes.

For further information

- Teach your students about online commerce – from Microsoft: <http://www.microsoft.com/office/previous/frontpage/columns/edcolumn04.asp>.
- European Commission form for seeking redress, available in 11 languages: <http://europa.eu.int/comm/consumers/redress/index_en.htm>.
- TRUSTe – an independent, non-profit, global initiative aimed at building trust and confidence in online transactions: <http://www.truste.org/>.
- UK Office of Fair Trading (OFT) information on online shopping: <http://www.oft.gov.uk/Consumer/Your+Rights+When+Shopping+From+Home/Online+shopping/default.htm>.
- European Commission page on e-commerce : <http://europa.eu.int/comm/internal_market/en/ecommerce/>.
- Amazon at <http://www.amazon.com>, and eBay at <http://www.ebay.com/> are two of the best known brands for online shopping.
- Paypal fraud prevention tips: <https://www.paypal.com/eBay/cgi-bin/webscr?cmd=p/gen/fraud-tips-buyers-outside>.
- "eBay 'most popular brand' online" – BBC article: <http://news.bbc.co.uk/2/hi/technology/4468745.stm>.
- Kelkoo is a website for comparing prices from different retailers: <http://fr.kelkoo.com/>.

Fact Sheet 19

Becoming an active e-citizen

Maintaining our rights as e-citizens

The widespread use of the Internet, and new communication technologies has been a powerful engine for growth and jobs and has improved the quality of life for many citizens.

The informed participation of all citizens in what is known as the digital economy depends on the development of a much broader literacy. This includes the ability to critically analyse the variety of information we are subject to (that is audiovisual content), to form autonomous opinions and to be actively involved in community issues.

What new skills are required for citizens to be active in society?

- Information and communication technologies are rapidly reaching into every aspect of our everyday lives and changing the type of skills necessary to be active members of society.
- As the Internet continues to evolve with the growth of wireless networks (http://en.wikipedia.org/wiki/Wireless_network) and 3G (http://en.wikipedia.org/wiki/ 3G) mobile technology), increasing importance will be placed on the ability to use today's technology to receive and transmit information efficiently in a way that transcends both media literacy and Internet literacy.

What advantages does the Internet offer in helping us become e-citizens?

- The Internet makes it possible not only to publish far more information more rapidly and to continually update this information so that citizens are informed of the latest developments in any areas of interest.
- In the past, we had to rely on the versions the press chose to publish to keep us informed; nowadays we can very often go directly to the source to obtain our information first hand.
- The fact that citizens are better informed empowers them to better participate in the democratic life of their own country and on a pan-European scale.
- Geographical, traffic, cultural and tourist information collected by public and private sector bodies considerably enriches the lives of citizens. In some countries, citizens can even use the Internet to officially change their address, apply for passport renewal or carry out various other formerly time-consuming activities. Do not forget, however, that a certain number of precautions should

be taken when giving out private information online (see Fact Sheets 15 and 16 on privacy and security).

- The Internet also enables citizens to participate in online discussions and debates about topics of interest in public or local life and even take part in elections by e-voting (http://en.wikipedia.org/wiki/E-voting).

Ethical issues on e-citizenship

By having access to constantly updated, quality information, citizens are in a better position to exercise their fundamental human rights. However, we must remain wary of the negative effects that technology could have on these rights, in particular:

- Equal access to information: the digital divide is creating a two-tier society between the information "haves" and "have-nots". If the situation continues, democracy will be threatened as the less fortunate gradually lose their autonomy of expression. Without direct access to information, we are less able to form our own opinion and can therefore be more easily manipulated by those who are fluent in the use of new technologies. In addition, public sector information is very important for democratic and civic life, and more particularly a key resource for economic activity. If we are to ensure equal opportunities for all, then we need to ensure equal information access for all.
- Freedom of speech: information and communication technologies are playing such an important role in our life today that soon only those fluent in their use will really be capable of making their "voice" heard.
- Right to privacy: the huge increase in means of transferring and exchanging information means that we must take care to protect data about ourselves and therefore our right to privacy (see "Best practice" below).

Ideas for classroom work

- Civics: One good resource which could serve as a basis for your civics study programme is the Council of Europe's online human rights activity programme at <http://www.hrea.org/erc/Library/First_Steps/index_eng.html>. You could also ask your class to draw up a human rights charter of its own. Let them apply their new knowledge about human rights to virtual environments, for example, how they could make the Internet a better place for them to work and play.
- History: the French revolution: Help your students to distinguish facts from hypothesis by comparing heroic revolutionary paintings of the storming of the Bastille with modern accounts. They should be able to "explain how and why the storming of the Bastille has been interpreted differently". This could be linked to media education concepts, such as how reality is represented for different purposes, and the reliability of evidence.
- Geography: passport to the world: Invite students to discuss the ways in which places of the world are represented on the Internet and analyse how the websites differ in emphasis or attitude with regard to a particular place.

- Content analysis: Choose a topic, and then look it up on news sites from different sources and analyse them in class. Do different organisations use different approaches? Why do you think this is so?

Best practice

- Every citizen has the right to receive a copy of personal information which is gathered and stored. Insist on this right, and do not give out private information unless you consider it necessary.
- Always read the fine print on questionnaires to see how the information you give about yourself is going to be used, and do not forget to consult Fact Sheet 15 on privacy for more advice.
- Communication of literacy skills and the transfer of these across school, higher education and into civic society is essential if participation in the democratic process is to increase.
- A number of schools are currently working on Internet proficiency programmes in an effort to ensure that their students develop the skills necessary to live, work and play in the information society of today. These include:

  - skills for navigating in the labyrinth of information available on the Internet;

  - developing the capacity to discriminate between information and misinformation;

  - analysing information for relevance and validity;

  - using information in project-based learning;

  - understanding and using the multiple opportunities that a browser and the Internet can offer.

For further information

- Amnesty International at <http://www.amnesty.org/> and Human Rights Watch at <http://www.hrw.org/> are non-governmental organisations that campaign for human rights. Amnesty has a multilingual manual that was designed for teachers to help young people learn about human rights, particularly in Central and Eastern Europe: <http://web.amnesty.org/web/web.nsf/pages/hre_first>.
- The European Commission has information on protecting children and human dignity in audiovisual services: <http://europa.eu.int/comm/avpolicy/regul/new_srv/pmhd_en.htm>.
- "They threw me a computer ... but what I really needed was a life preserver", article in First Monday, a peer-reviewed journal on the Internet, identifies four attributes of the digital divide – literacy, access, content and training – and discusses the role of libraries and museums in cultivating each of these capacities: <http://www.firstmonday.dk/issues/issue6_4/wilhelm/index.html>.

- Globalizing Democracy: <http://www.prospect.org/print/V11/20/barber-b.html>.
- Article "The responsive classroom: a practical approach for bringing democratic ideals into the daily fabric of classroom life": <http://www.newhorizons.org/strategies/democratic/gimbert.htm>.

Fact Sheet 20

Mobile technology

Introduction

Few people bought mobile phones when they first became available in 1983. In 1995, there were five mobile subscriptions per 100 inhabitants in the European Union. According to Eurostat (2005), in 2003 the figure was 80 mobile phones per 100 inhabitants among the enlarged EU of 25 countries. Mobile phone usage is a worldwide phenomenon, growing fastest in Africa.

Standard features of mobile phones are voice calls and short message service (SMS) (http://en.wikipedia.org/wiki/Short_message_service). So-called "smart-phones" have new capabilities such as e-mail, picture messaging and video.

The worlds of mobile technology and personal computing are becoming less and less distinct as many mobile phones now have Internet browsing and e-mail capabilities, and more and more computers are wireless.

Education

- M-learning refers to learning with the aid of mobile technologies, such as mobile phones, handheld computers and PDAs.
- SRI International research in 2003 found that 90% of teachers who had used mobile technology found it contributed positively to student learning: <http://www.intel.com/ education/handhelds/SRI.pdf>.
- M-learning offers the possibility to personalise the teaching delivered to students. For example, a school in the United States has set up a "paperless classroom",– using the technology to give classes and provide extra assistance to those who have English as a second language: <http://www.paperlessclassroom.org/>.
- The future of m-learning depends not only on the development of technology, but also the development of educational material that can be delivered over handheld devices.
- Korea is recognised as one of the pioneers in mobile learning. Since 2004, students have been able to download lectures to handheld mobile devices.
- Games for mobile phones are becoming increasingly popular as the technology improves and it is anticipated that educational games and other types of informal learning will be well-suited to the medium.

- The portability of handheld computers is beneficial for teachers who are on the move and for students working in groups or doing fieldwork
- Use of handheld computers has been found to encourage students to take responsibility for their work and they are less likely to lose notes and assignments.
- Since mobile phones are so popular with young people, teachers can engage students by incorporating use of SMSs and so forth in classroom activities.

Issues

- There are concerns about children receiving mobiles too early. Research is inconclusive about the dangers of radiation exposure over time, however minimal.
- Computer use is still regulated within the home. Mobile phone use, however is considered by many parents to be private. Emboldened by newfound freedom, children could get themselves into financial trouble by spending money on prize "giveaway" media campaigns or accessories such as ringtones.
- Mobiles may be used as tracking devices. The issue of safety versus freedom is a controversial one.
- Bluetooth technology (http://en.wikipedia.org/wiki/Bluetooth) raises security issues such as hacking and sending unsolicited messages.
- Moblogs (http://en.wikipedia.org/wiki/Moblog) are mobile phone blogs (web diaries). Young people are posting information and photos and potentially compromising their safety.
- Mobile bullying is of growing concern. Young people called "happy slappers" (http://en.wikipedia.org/wiki/Happy_slapping) use mobile phones to record attacks and then post the images on the Web to humiliate the victim. This takes place mostly in the United Kingdom (see Fact Sheet 17 on bullying and harassment).
- Because they are a distraction, mobiles can pose a risk while driving.
- Viruses (http://en.wikipedia.org/wiki/Computer_virus) and worms (http://en.wikipedia.org/wiki/Computer_worm) have been infecting mobiles since 2004. One example is the "Cabir worm".

How to

- Mobile phones are popular and it is easy and relatively inexpensive to own one.
- Once you buy a handset you can choose to pay a-la-carte for certain increments of minutes or you can subscribe to a specific provider and pay a monthly fee for services.

Best practice

- Encourage young people to restrict their use of mobile phones. Do not prohibit use, however. Mobile phone use is a widespread phenomenon among teens and in many circles it is essential for networking among peers.

- Do not leave Bluetooth on if it is not being used in order to avoid security risks.
- As with e-mail, accept data only from trusted sources.
- Be considerate with your use of the phone. People around you may not appreciate having to listen to your conversation.

For further information

- The e-Learning Centre's m-Learning page: <http://www.e-learningcentre.co.uk/eclipse/Resources/mlearning.htm>.
- Independent UK site for reviewing mobile phones: <http://www.mobile-phones-uk.org.uk/>.
- Literature Review in Mobile Technologies and Learning – a detailed University of Birmingham report including case studies and a view for the future of mobile learning: <http://www.nestafuturelab.org/research/reviews/reviews_11_and12/11_01.htm>.
- M-learning is a research and development programme investigating mobile learning among young people at risk of social exclusion: <http://www.m-learning.org/>.
- Wireless world forum: <http://www.w2forum.com/>
- Children and mobile phones, an agenda for action", online publication by Childnet International: <http://www.childnet-int.org/downloads/CMPAAA_A4.pdf>.
- Independent Mobile Classification Body (IMCB): <http://www.imcb.org.uk/>
- Mobile Data Association (MDA): <http://www.mda-mobiledata.org/mda/>.
- Nokia page on protecting your phone from Bluetooth and malware: <http://europe.nokia.com/nokia/0,,76016,00.html>.
- Bluetooth's security page: <http://www.bluetooth.com/help/security.asp>.
- Mobile operator Vodafone's guide for parents: <http://www.vodafone.co.uk/download/CSR%20Parent%20guide.pdf>.

Fact Sheet 21

Blogs

Introduction

- The word "blog" (http://en.wikipedia.org/wiki/Blog) is short for "weblog", and refers to an online journal created and published by groups and individuals.
- The term "weblog" was added to the Oxford dictionary in 2003. Blogs are a recent phenomenon on the Internet.
- Because bloggers post articles and information online, this trend has begun to take over a lot of newsgroup traffic (see Fact Sheet 8 on newsgroups).
- Although some politicians and celebrities have taken up blogging, blogs continue to be most closely associated with more ordinary people airing their views and talking about their daily lives.
- Because of the recent popularity of blogs, many websites have been created which offer software to help create and publish material. Each entry in a blog can be commented upon, which provides opportunities for discussion and can help generate new ideas. Mobile blogs, known as moblogs (http://en.wikipedia.org/wiki/Moblogging), have recently emerged thanks to development of e-mail features in mobile phones (see Fact Sheet 20 on mobile technology).
- Vlogging (http://en.wikipedia.org/wiki/Vlog) is a new trend in which users post video along with their commentary.
- RSS (http://en.wikipedia.org/wiki/RSS_%28file_format%29) or rich site summary is now being used to syndicate blogs. Those who wish to have their content published on other websites can make it available using an XML (http://en.wikipedia.org/ wiki/XML) or extensible mark-up language version for web syndication. XML is a type of code similar to HTML and is also known as a "feed". Basically it allows readers to "subscribe" to content and have blog updates delivered to them so that they do not have to visit the blog to get it. This sounds complicated but is actually a standard option on most blogging software.

Educational uses of blogging

- Blogs give students a chance to take control of their learning and set up a public forum in which to publish their thoughts and feelings.
- Blogs can be used as an innovative teaching tool for discussion and collaboration. For example, a modern literature class used blogging to study the novel

The secret life of bees (http://weblogs.hcrhs.k12.nj.us/bees/). The author wrote an introduction to the lesson and students and their parents were invited to write about their impressions of each day's reading assignment. The author then commented on these. See: <http://weblogs. hcrhs.k12.nj.us/bees/>.

- Experts note a three-step process involved when blogging. This is described at <http://www.thejournal.com/magazine/vault/A4677C.cfm>. Bloggers must continually scour, filter and post material. By searching for material to comment on, the student becomes increasingly familiar with different theories and ideas and develops skills needed to critically analyse content.
- Technology can be used as a motivating factor in education. Students are interested in blogs because of their novelty and the possibilities for self-expression. This can be used as a vehicle to teach a wide variety of subject matter.
- Blogs give every student in the class a chance to participate in a discussion which exposes children to different perspectives.

Ethical considerations and risks

- Remind students that they should not give out personal information in public Internet spaces. This is a particular problem with blogs, which are often personal by their very nature.

How to

- If you have the technical skills, you can create a blog from scratch. Most people use sites which offer tools for creating and publishing content as a blog. School Blogs at <http://www.schoolblogs.com/> and Blogger (see below) are popular hosts which provide free services. They provide easy, step-by-step instructions which help you create an account, name your blog and choose a template.
- Once your blog is up and running, you compose and edit entries from a central webpage. The interface for popular software is WYSIWYG (http://en. wikipedia.org/ wiki/WYSIWYG) format and is extremely user-friendly.
- Visitors to your blog can comment on content by clicking on a comments link at the end of each entry.
- Be sure to enrich your commentary with hyperlinks and images! Buttons for these features should be included on the toolbar above the text box where you enter your content.

Best practice

- A blog is a great opportunity to air your views but you may wish to protect your privacy by using a pseudonym and holding back certain personal details.
- Children and young people should be particularly careful about revealing personal information in a blog.
- Respect copyright laws and do not use other people's blog designs without their permission.

- Start your own blog to familiarise yourself with the practice before introducing it into the classroom. It might help to visit other blogs for ideas and inspiration. The School Blogs (http://www.schoolblogs.com/) website has more than 4 000 members and gives users the possibility to launch their own school blog.
- Spend time explaining the concept of blogging to your students. Tell them why it is done and give examples of good and bad blogs. Then give students a set of strict rules which might include length and frequency of posts, topics, number of hyperlinks/photos and so forth. Assign students to keep a blog, discuss their experiences and comment on others' blogs.

For further information

- Blogger is a site providing tools for blogging and now moblogging: <http://www.blogger.com/start>.
- 14 copyright tips for bloggers: <http://weblogs.about.com/od/issuesanddiscussions/a/copyrighttips.htm>.
- Electronic Frontiers Foundation (EFF) legal guide for bloggers: <http://www.eff.org/bloggers/lg/>.
- Dartmouth college tips for online classroom discussions: <http://www.dartmouth.edu/~webteach/articles/discussion.html>.
- BBC article of 23 January 2005 "Academics give lessons on blogs": <http://news.bbc.co.uk/2/hi/uk_news/education/4194669.stm>.
- Weblogg-ed – this site follows current blogging trends in education: <http://www.weblogg-ed.com/>.
- Article in Journal, February 2004, "Content Delivery in the Blogosphere": <http://www.thejournal.com/magazine/vault/A4677.cfm>.
- Blogging and RSS – the "What's It?" and "How To" of Powerful New Web Tools for Educators: <http://www.infotoday.com/MMSchools/jan04/richardson.shtml>.
- Educational Weblogs: <http://educational.blogs.com/>.
- The Educated Blogger: Using Weblogs to promote literacy in the classroom: <http://firstmonday.org/issues/issue9_6/huffaker/>.
- Tools to Support K-12 Student Writing: <http://www.cesa12.k12.wi.us/teach/write/blogs.html>.
- Blog Idea File: list of ways that teachers are using blogs: <http://www.weblogg-ed.com/stories/storyReader$100>.
- Blogging resources for educators: <http://www3.essdack.org/socialstudies/blogs.htm>.

Sales agents for publications of the Council of Europe
Agents de vente des publications du Conseil de l'Europe

BELGIUM/BELGIQUE
La Librairie européenne SA
Rue de l'Orme 1
1040 BRUXELLES
Tel.: (32) 2 231 04 35
Fax: (32) 2 735 08 60
E-mail:mail@libeurop.be
http://www.libeurop.be

Jean de Lannoy
202, avenue du Roi
B-1190 BRUXELLES
Tel.: (32) 2 538 4308
Fax: (32) 2 538 0841
E-mail: jean.de.lannoy@euronet.be
http://www.jean-de-lannoy.be

CANADA
Renouf Publishing Company Limited
5369 Chemin Canotek Road
CDN-OTTAWA, Ontario, K1J 9J3
Tel.: (1) 613 745 2665
Fax: (1) 613 745 7660
E-mail: order.dept@renoufbooks.com
http://www.renoufbooks.com

CZECH REPUBLIC/ RÉPUBLIQUE TCHÈQUE
Suweco Cz Dovoz Tisku Praha
Ceskomoravska 21
CZ-18021 PRAHA 9
Tel.: (420) 2 660 35 364
Fax: (420) 2 683 30 42
E-mail: import@suweco.cz

DENMARK/DANEMARK
GAD Direct
Fiolstaede 31-33
DK-1171 COPENHAGEN K
Tel.: (45) 33 13 72 33
Fax: (45) 33 12 54 94
E-mail: info@gaddirect.dk

FINLAND/FINLANDE
Akateeminen Kirjakauppa
Keskuskatu 1, PO Box 218
FIN-00381 HELSINKI
Tel.: (358) 9 121 41
Fax: (358) 9 121 4450
E-mail: akatilaus@stockmann.fi
http://www.akatilaus.akateeminen.com

FRANCE
La Documentation française
(Diffusion/Vente France entière)
124, rue H. Barbusse
F-93308 AUBERVILLIERS Cedex
Tel.: (33) 01 40 15 70 00
Fax: (33) 01 40 15 68 00
E-mail: commandes.vel@ladocfrancaise.gouv.fr
http://www.ladocfrancaise.gouv.fr

Librairie Kléber (Vente Strasbourg)
Palais de l'Europe
F-67075 STRASBOURG Cedex
Fax: (33) 03 88 52 91 21
E-mail: librairie.kleber@coe.int

GERMANY/ALLEMAGNE AUSTRIA/AUTRICHE
August Bebel Allee 6
Am Hofgarten 10
D-53175 BONN
Tel.: (49) 2 28 94 90 20
Fax: (49) 2 28 94 90 222
E-mail: bestellung@uno-verlag.de
http://www.uno-verlag.de

GREECE/GRÈCE
Librairie Kauffmann
28, rue Stadiou
GR-ATHINAI 10564
Tel.: (30) 1 32 22 160
Fax: (30) 1 32 30 320
E-mail: ord@otenet.gr

HUNGARY/HONGRIE
Euro Info Service
Hungexpo Europa Kozpont ter 1
H-1101 BUDAPEST
Tel.: (361) 264 8270
Fax: (361) 264 8271
E-mail: euroinfo@euroinfo.hu
http://www.euroinfo.hu

ITALY/ITALIE
Libreria Commissionaria Sansoni
Via Duca di Calabria 1/1, CP 552
I-50125 FIRENZE
Tel.: (39) 556 4831
Fax: (39) 556 41257
E-mail: licosa@licosa.com
http://www.licosa.com

NETHERLANDS/PAYS-BAS
De Lindeboom Internationale Publikaties
PO Box 202, MA de Ruyterstraat 20 A
NL-7480 AE HAAKSBERGEN
Tel.: (31) 53 574 0004
Fax: (31) 53 572 9296
E-mail: books@delindeboom.com
http://www.delindeboom.com

NORWAY/NORVÈGE
Akademika, A/S Universitetsbokhandel
PO Box 84, Blindern
N-0314 OSLO
Tel.: (47) 22 85 30 30
Fax: (47) 23 12 24 20

POLAND/POLOGNE
Głowna Księgarnia Naukowa
im. B. Prusa
Krakowskie Przedmiescie 7
PL-00-068 WARSZAWA
Tel.: (48) 29 22 66
Fax: (48) 22 26 64 49
E-mail: inter@internews.com.pl
http://www.internews.com.pl

PORTUGAL
Livraria Portugal
Rua do Carmo, 70
P-1200 LISBOA
Tel.: (351) 13 47 49 82
Fax: (351) 13 47 02 64
E-mail: liv.portugal@mail.telepac.pt

SPAIN/ESPAGNE
Mundi-Prensa Libros SA
Castelló 37
E-28001 MADRID
Tel.: (34) 914 36 37 00
Fax: (34) 915 75 39 98
E-mail: libreria@mundiprensa.es
http://www.mundiprensa.com

SWITZERLAND/SUISSE
Adeco – Van Diermen
Chemin du Lacuez 41
CH-1807 BLONAY
Tel.: (41) 21 943 26 73
Fax: (41) 21 943 36 05
E-mail: info@adeco.org

UNITED KINGDOM/ROYAUME-UNI
TSO (formerly HMSO)
51 Nine Elms Lane
GB-LONDON SW8 5DR
Tel.: (44) 207 873 8372
Fax: (44) 207 873 8200
E-mail: customer.services@theso.co.uk
http://www.the-stationery-office.co.uk
http://www.itsofficial.net

UNITED STATES and CANADA/ ÉTATS-UNIS et CANADA
Manhattan Publishing Company
2036 Albany Post Road
CROTON-ON-HUDSON,
NY 10520, USA
Tel.: (1) 914 271 5194
Fax: (1) 914 271 5856
E-mail: Info@manhattanpublishing.com
http://www.manhattanpublishing.com

Council of Europe Publishing/Editions du Conseil de l'Europe
F-67075 Strasbourg Cedex
Tel.: (33) 03 88 41 25 81 – Fax: (33) 03 88 41 39 10 – E-mail: publishing@coe.int – Website: http://book.coe.int